THE
JOHANNINE EPISTLES

EPWORTH PREACHER'S COMMENTARIES

*

THE
JOHANNINE EPISTLES

*

GREVILLE P. LEWIS
B.A., B.D.

LONDON : THE EPWORTH PRESS

FIRST PUBLISHED IN 1961

© THE EPWORTH PRESS 1961

Book Steward
FRANK H. CUMBERS

SET IN MONOTYPE TIMES ROMAN AND PRINTED IN
GREAT BRITAIN BY THE CAMELOT PRESS LTD
LONDON AND SOUTHAMPTON

To the memory of
WILBERT FRANCIS HOWARD
to whom, as scholar and friend,
I owe so much

General Introduction

WE are living in a day in which the authority and message of the Bible are being rediscovered and declared. Preachers are realizing afresh that their message must be based on the Word of God in Scripture. Many commentaries on the books of the Bible are already available, and give much space to the consideration of critical questions and historical and literary problems.

This new series of commentaries, as its name suggests, is written specifically for preachers, and particularly for those who feel themselves ill-equipped to study the more advanced works of scholarship. Its aim is to set forth the essential message of the Bible. Questions of authorship, date, background, etc., will be dealt with briefly, and only in so far as they are necessary for informed preaching. The main purpose of each commentary will be (a) to explain the original meaning of each biblical passage, and (b) to indicate its relevance to human need in the present situation. Bearing in mind this dual purpose, each author will have freedom to use what method of treatment he thinks most suitable to the book of the Bible on which he is commenting.

To save space, the biblical text is not printed, but the commentary is based on that of the *Revised Version*.

The writer of the present Commentary is the General Editor of the *Epworth Preacher's Commentaries*. On the insistence of the New Testament editors, and in a moment of weakness, he consented to move from the editor's chair to the author's desk. After more than thirty years as an ordinary minister, followed by twelve years as Secretary of the Local Preachers Department of the Methodist Church, he can perhaps claim to have some understanding of the *needs* of the average preacher, ministerial and lay, in the matter of commentaries. As he expected, however, he has discovered that it is easier to explain these needs to the writers of other Preacher's Commentaries than to try to meet them by writing one himself. In future, the General Editor may be a little less exacting when he deals with his fellow-commentators.

GREVILLE P. LEWIS

Preface

SINCE the Johannine Epistles contain only seven chapters, some explanation of the size of this commentary is needed. (a) Most of the great themes in the Johannine Epistles are derived from (and cannot be fully understood apart from) the teaching of our Lord as recorded in the Gospel of John. This commentary would therefore have been considerably shorter if I had been able to give cross-references to the commentary on John's Gospel in this series. Because that commentary has not yet been published, I have often found it necessary to summarize the teaching of the Gospel on a particular theme before I could comment on John's references to that theme in the Epistles. (b) As the General Introduction says, one main purpose of these Preacher's Commentaries is to help the expository preacher to show that the Bible speaks to every age, and that its essential message meets the deepest needs of the men and women of today. In the hope that he will welcome it, I have given the preacher more expository material than could be given by an author who is commenting on a larger book of the Bible.

I am deeply indebted to many friends for their ungrudging help. In my early ministry I was privileged to be a member of the Birmingham New Testament Seminar, of which Dr Wilbert F. Howard was the secretary and under whose scholarly leadership we studied the Gospel of John for three exciting years. During the next twenty years, as from time to time I returned to the study of that Gospel, Dr Howard often shared with me his profound knowledge of the Johannine Writings. When Prof. C. H. Dodd published his *Moffatt Commentary* on the Johannine Epistles, I raised certain questions with him, and I shall always be grateful to him for his courteous and helpful letters. My cordial thanks are also due to Prof. C. Kingsley Barrett for his guidance in matters of exegesis when I was out of my depth, and to the New Testament editors, Dr C. Leslie Mitton and Kenneth Grayston, for their frank and constructive criticisms. Ministers' wives—and especially those whose husbands write books in their spare time—are a long-suffering race; outstanding among them, by virtue of her cheerful tolerance of 'that commentary' and her unfailing encouragement of the writer of it, is the gracious lady who shares my life and home.

EASTBOURNE   GREVILLE P. LEWIS

Abbreviations

EVV.   English Versions (*AV* and *RV*).
RSV.   *Revised Standard Version.*
AEB.   A. E. Brooke, *The Johannine Epistles* (I.C.C.).
CHD.   C. H. Dodd, *The Johannine Epistles* (Moffatt Commentaries).
GGF.   G. G. Findlay, *Fellowship in the Life Eternal.*
WFH.   W. F. Howard, *Christianity according to St John.*
CLM.   C. Leslie Mitton, *St Mark* (E.P.C.).
KG.   Kenneth Grayston, *Galatians and Philippians* (E.P.C.)
MHB.   *The Methodist Hymnbook* (1933).

N.B. Text references printed in heavy type, as 3^{10}, relate to chapters and verses in *1 John.*

First Epistle of John

Introduction

The Author

IN view of the close relationship between John's Gospel and the Johannine Epistles, a commentator cannot discuss the authorship of the Epistles without expressing his judgement, however briefly, on the authorship of the Gospel. In doing so, I can only summarize my own conclusions, without giving the reasons for them or the objections which can be raised against them—as follows: (*a*) Behind the Fourth Gospel are the witness and authority of *the apostle John*, 'the disciple whom Jesus loved', whose intimacy with Jesus was such that he understood our Lord's person and teaching as no other man did, and who seems to have accompanied Jesus on His various journeys to Jerusalem. In his preaching, he gave to the Church in Palestine his reminiscences and interpretations of the ministry of Jesus and, after A.D. 70 and the dispersal of the Christians, he went (via Antioch?) to Ephesus where, perhaps, he committed his memoirs to writing ('wrote these things', Jn. 21²⁴). Here he died in old age. (*b*) The actual author of the Gospel was a *disciple of the apostle*, a native of Jerusalem who emigrated with his master to Ephesus. There is evidence in the Gospel that (in his youth) he himself had seen something of the ministry of Jesus in Jerusalem, and this would explain '*we* beheld' in John 1¹⁴. He used the teaching (and written memoirs?) of the apostle as the main source of the Gospel. In John 19³⁵ he vouched for the reliability of the apostle as an eye-witness ('he knoweth' = 'the author knoweth'), and in John 21²⁴ his colleagues at Ephesus joined him in adding a further guarantee. One of his purposes in writing the Gospel was to present the person and work of Jesus Christ in a way which would appeal to the Hellenists of Asia Minor.

It is generally agreed that the man who wrote John's Gospel also wrote *1 John*. The phraseology and style of the two writings, the themes with which they deal, and the theological point of view which distinguishes them from all the other New Testament writings give an immediate impression of identity of authorship (*AEB*, pp. i-xix). In his *Moffatt Commentary*, C. H. Dodd is so impressed by the differences in style and thought that he concludes that *1 John* was written by a *disciple* of the author of the Gospel (*CHD*, pp. xlvii-lvi). There are certainly differences of emphasis between the theology of *1 John* and the distinctive thought of the Gospel, and these will be mentioned in the course of the commentary, but W. F. Howard's reply to the arguments of Prof. Dodd seems to confirm the widely held view that the same man wrote both the Gospel and the First Epistle (*The Fourth Gospel in Recent Criticism*, revised by C. K. Barrett [1955], pp. 282-95). If so, it is the same man who writes '*we beheld*' in John 1[14] and 1[1].

There can be little doubt that the author of *1 John* is the author of *2 and 3 John*, who calls himself 'The Elder' or 'The Presbyter' (2 Jn 1, 3 Jn 1), a title which, at the end of the first century, was given to men who were disciples of the apostles. In one of his books (quoted by Eusebius), Papias (*c.* 60-130), bishop of Hierapolis in Asia Minor, distinguished between two Johns; the apostle John, and 'Presbyter John' who outlived him. Is this 'the Elder' of Ephesus who wrote both the Gospel and the Epistles? If so, we may speak of 'The Gospel according to John the apostle, as written by John the elder', just as we may speak of 'The Gospel according to Peter, as written by Mark'; and we may speak of 'the Epistles of John'—the Elder.

John is widely known and revered as '*the* Elder' throughout the Roman province of Asia. He writes as their recognized pastor to his 'little children', his dearly loved flock in his widespread 'diocese'. He is deeply concerned about their spiritual welfare, their doctrinal fidelity and their ethical conduct. He sends missionaries on evangelistic tours to distant areas, and sees that discipline is maintained in the local churches. In a word, as one who had seen the Lord and been a disciple of the apostle John, he exercises an authority which was similar to that of the Bishop of Ephesus a few decades later (see Introduction to *3 John*, p. 133).

The Date

The Epistles were probably written a year or two *after* the Gospel. Again and again, in such condensed passages as

2[3-8], John seems to take it for granted that his readers are familiar with his fuller exposition of such themes in his Gospel. He is writing what might almost be called the first Commentary on the Gospel, to stress, and help his 'children' to understand, its basic message. Until recently the Gospel was thought to have been written *c.* A.D. 95-100, but for a number of reasons many scholars are now inclined to date it *c.* 85. If John was a young man at the end of Christ's ministry, and if the Gospel has written *c.* 85 and the Epistles *c.* 87, the Elder would be about 75 years old when he wrote the Epistles—not too old to have done so, or to make the journeys anticipated in *3 John*. When he wrote, Christianity was unpopular in Asia Minor (**3**[13]), but the hostility of Emperor Domitian to the Church did not break out in fierce persecution until A.D. 95, about which time *Revelation* was published. In *1-2 John* the antichrist is not Rome and Caesar-worship, but Gnostic heresy, and in *3 John* the problem is not persecution from without, but indiscipline within the Church. The date *c.* A.D. 87 seems to fit such a situation.

The Purpose

The First Epistle is a pastoral letter, not addressed to any particular circle of believers, but intended for general publication among all the churches of the 'diocese'. It had a twofold purpose.

(*a*) *To refute dangerous heresy*. When the early Christian missionaries took the gospel into Asia Minor and eastern Europe, they soon came into contact with a new religious movement among the pagan intellectuals of the Mediterranean world. It was an age of speculation about the nature of God, the origin of evil and the destiny of the human soul; an age in which most thinking people had abandoned belief in the old gods of Greece and Rome. Many of them were now experimenting with one of the various forms of that New Paganism which we may describe as Early Gnosticism. (The word comes from the Greek '*gnosis*' which means 'knowledge'.) Behind this movement was the conviction that there is some truth in all religions and philosophies, and that it was possible to combine such truths into a new and *universal* religion. In our own day, Theosophy makes a similar claim, and may be regarded as the lineal descendant of Gnosticism. When converts from

paganism to Christianity came under the influence of this first-
century Theosophy, some of them were attracted by its daring
speculations, its mysticism, its search for a universal religion
and its offer of salvation without any stern ethical demands.
By comparison, the apostolic faith seemed crude and exacting,
though it contained sublime ideas which could be made the
basis of a more imposing and satisfying theology. So they began
to *reinterpret* Christianity in line with the alien presuppositions
of this 'modern thought' in an attempt to show that the
Christian faith could be so presented as to satisfy the search
of the Gnostic intellectuals for 'salvation by knowledge'.

About 30 years before *1 John* was written in Ephesus,
Paul had to warn the church at near-by Colossae against a
'higher thought' heresy which seems to have been an earlier
form of 'Christian' Gnosticism (Col 2^{8-9}, $^{18-19}$; cf. 1 Cor 13^2)
and at a later date, in 1 Timothy 6^{20}, he told Timothy to beware of 'profane babblings' and of 'knowledge which is falsely
so called'. Towards the end of the century, however, the heresy
in the Ephesus 'diocese' was much more serious and disruptive.
That is why John so vigorously exposes its errors in *1 John*,
and makes it clear that those who hold these false opinions
have no right to call themselves Christians. What these
heretics believed and taught we shall discover as we study the
letter, for every now and then John quotes one of their Gnostic
catch-phrases (see comments on $1^{6, \ 8, \ 10}$, $2^{4, \ 6, \ 9, \ 22}$, 4^{20}). To
what extent they threatened the fellowship and witness of the
Church we shall see when we study 2^{19}, $4^{1, \ 5}$.

(*b*) *To establish the faith of the immature.* John's main concern is with the rank and file of the Church who, so far, have
remained loyal to apostolic Christianity. Some of them are
unsettled by the arguments of the heretical intellectuals. Might
it be true that the simple gospel as taught by John and his
colleagues was rather old-fashioned and elementary? Others
were second-generation Christians; they had accepted the
Christian faith from their parents, and not as a result of personal conviction and conversion. Their faith was immature,
and perhaps they were finding increasingly irksome the moral
demands of the gospel and the tensions between the discipline
of the Church and the attractions of pagan society. John writes
to remind these weaker brethren of the unalterable funda-
mentals of the faith, and to give them certain practical tests
by which they may *know* whether or not they are in that real

and saving relationship with God through Christ which is 'eternal life'. He sums up this purpose in 5^{13}.

Since A.D. 81, when Domitian was crowned emperor, it must have been obvious that a fierce persecution of the Church might break out at any time. It is a remarkable fact that John almost completely ignores this threat; see comment on 2^{18}.

Basic Assumptions of the Early Gnostics

(*a*) *Dualism*. Greek dualism was the belief that the universe is divided into the upper world of spirit which is essentially good, and the lower world of matter which is essentially evil. Persian dualism was the belief that there are two eternal and opposing deities in the universe, the god of light and goodness, and the god of darkness and evil. By combining Greek and Persian dualism, the Gnostics sought to solve the unsolvable problem of the origin of evil. They held that God, who is pure spirit, could not possibly make any contact with this evil material world, which is for ever under the control of the Devil.

(*b*) *Creation*. It follows that God could not have created this evil material world. What He did was to put forth a series of 'emanations' to rule over the spaces between heaven and earth. Each 'emanation' in this series was farther from God than the preceding one, and the last one (sometimes called the Demiurge) was so far from God, and therefore so unspiritual, that he was able to make contact with matter. This Demiurge was the Creator of the material world. He was not only ignorant of God, but was actually hostile to Him.

(*c*) *Salvation*. The rational or spiritual part of man (his soul) is a spark emanating from God, but it is imprisoned in a body which is part of the evil material world. Thus man is cut off from the upper world of spirit and light. The problem of his salvation is *how* he can escape from the dark dungeon of the body, and make his way into the realm of pure light. The Gnostics taught that a secret knowledge about God and the spirit world was brought down from heaven by a Revealer (or 'light-bringer'), and was imparted to certain elect souls (Note that limitation) by means of mystical experiences or mysterious sacraments. By this secret enlightenment, the privileged few could safely ascend past the 'emanations' who ruled and guarded the successive spheres between earth and heaven, each new revelation of truth bringing him nearer to the spirit world.

B

Finally the elect would reach and be united with (or rather absorbed into) the godhead, and so become deified, i.e. saved. So, to the Gnostics, salvation was not from sin, but from ignorance, and through privately revealed knowledge of the spirit world. Also, since the 'emanations' which rule the spaces between heaven and earth were sometimes identified with the sun, the moon and the planets, who were supposed to influence the destiny of human beings, this ascent into the upper world could also be regarded as salvation from fate.

The form of the Letter

It is impossible to discover a clear scheme of thought in the First Epistle; in a personal letter, Dr C. Kingsley Barrett comments: 'A very bad model for a preacher.' As R. Law and others have pointed out, John's thought seems to move in a series of spirals. He does not deal with his master themes one by one, developing his message and drawing his conclusions. He takes a series of related themes, meditates around them, and then drops them—only to return to them, again and again, later in the letter, on each occasion adding something to what he has already said about each of them. So, he deals with the Person of Christ in $1^{1-3, 7}$, 2^{22-3}, 3^{23}, $4^{2, 15}$, $5^{1, 5, 20}$; with eternal life in 1^2, 2^{25}, 3^{14-15}, 4^9, 5^{20}; with knowledge of God in $2^{3-4, 13-14}$, 3^6, 4^{7-8}, 5^{20}; and so on. In the hope that it will help the preacher, I have summarized and commented on most of John's great themes in a series of twenty-seven *Notes*, to which I have given numerous cross-references in the course of the commentary.

Commentary

1^{1-4}. PREFACE TO THE EPISTLE

Summary: *My theme is the gospel of Eternal Life—that original gospel which centres in Jesus Christ who is the Life, and who revealed it in an incarnate life on earth, as we eye-witnesses testify to you. Only the message of this gospel can maintain the unity of the Church.*

As we have seen, *1 John* is a pastoral tract, rather than a personal letter. Instead of the greetings to readers with which Paul began his letters, John begins his tract, as he ends it

(5^{20-1}), with a striking summary of his main theme. Compare it with the Prologue to his Gospel.

Before we examine this long and complicated sentence, we must ask what John means by '*the word of life*' in verse 1. It is '*concerning*' this, he says, that he is writing; this is his master theme. At first glance the phrase looks like a direct reference to the Prologue of the Gospel, in which Christ is described as '*the Word*' who was in '*the beginning*' with God, in whom was '*life*', and who became flesh so that men '*beheld*' His glory (Jn $1^{1, 4, 14}$). If so, '*the word of life*' is a description of Christ, as in the Revised Version and Moffatt. But only in Jn 1^1 is Christ called 'the Word', and nowhere else in the New Testament is He called '*the word of life*'. It is more probable that John uses the phrase as it was used by Paul in Philippians 2^{16} ('Holding forth *the word of life*', where 'the word' means 'the gospel'); cf. Acts 5^{20}, where 'the words of this life' means 'this gospel of life'. In other New Testament passages, 'the word' means 'the gospel', as in Acts 13^{26}, 20^{32}, 1 Corinthians 1^{18}, 2 Corinthians 5^{19}. A comparison of Philippians 2^{16} and Acts 5^{20} with John 6^{68} ('Thou hast the words of eternal life') adds force to the suggestion that '*concerning the word of life*' means 'concerning the gospel of life'; that is, 'concerning the gospel which centres in Christ who *is* the life, and who *gives* life to all who will receive it'. That is John's theme, and that is the theme of all our preaching.

Now let us look at the whole paragraph. Ignoring verse 2 which is bracketed as an 'aside', the main sentence reads: '*That which was from the beginning, that which we have heard . . ., concerning the word of life . . . declare we unto you.*' What we declare unto you, says John, is that which, '*from the beginning*' was true about the gospel of life. In 2^{13-14}, this phrase refers to the '*beginning*' of the universe; but in $2^{7, 24}$, 3^{11} it refers to the 'beginning' of the preaching of the gospel. Here John probably has both these meanings in mind. The gospel is an eternal gospel. It was in God's mind when He first created humanity; was revealed as He worked out His saving purposes in the history of His chosen people, the Hebrews: and it was lived out, and so came to its supreme climax, in the earthly ministry of Jesus His Son. The heretics of his day said that the faith of the Church was out-dated by their 'new theology'. John flung back his answer: the true, unchanging gospel goes back to Bethelehem and Galilee and Jerusalem—

no, back to the beginning of history—and no 'revised version' of it is needed or is genuine.

But the Christians of John's 'diocese' were disturbed by the arguments of the primitive 'Christian Gnostics' (see p. 5) who minimized the importance of the historical life of Jesus and even denied the fact of the Incarnation. In this opening sentence, therefore, John states in positive terms the basic truth on which the Christian faith is grounded, and at the same time launches a robust counter-attack against these critics of orthodox Christianity. '*We have heard*'; '*we have seen*'; '*we beheld*' (that is, we carefully observed, so as to grasp its significance); '*handled*'; '*manifested*'. In all these phrases in 1^{1-3}, John stresses the vital truth that Christianity is not (like Gnosticism) a system of philosophical speculations about God and life, but is a historical religion; that God's revelation of Himself as the God of light and love and the Saviour of men has been expressed in a series of mighty acts throughout the history of the Hebrew people, and now has actually been lived out on earth in the incarnate life of His own Son, Jesus Christ. This startling truth is the very foundation of the Christian faith, and it dominates John's thought in this epistle (see *Note 1*, p. 15).

The actual facts of the life of Jesus—His birth, ministry, death and resurrection—and the apostolic interpretation of those facts, had already been recorded in the Gospels of Mark, Matthew and Luke, and more recently in John's own Gospel, and the Christians of Asia Minor were familiar with them through the preaching- and teaching-ministry of the Church. These facts, writes John, are authentic and incontrovertible; they are affirmed by the personal evidence of reliable eye-witnesses. Both the facts which they guarantee, and the firm conclusions about them which they reached, will be accepted by all true believers.

But who are these eye-witnesses who are referred to as '*we*' in 1^{1-2}? When John wrote, the last of the apostles, John the son of Zebedee, had died. But we have seen (p. 1) that there is evidence that the Elder himself had been a personal observer of at least the closing months of Jesus's ministry in Jerusalem. John, therefore, includes himself among those disciples of Jesus who had been the eye-witnesses of His ministry—the Twelve, the Seventy, the ministering women, Nicodemus, Joseph of Arimathea, the owners of the colt and of the upper room, and the rest of them. '*We*', he says. '*We have heard*' Jesus proclaim the gospel of God and '*we*', too, were able to say with Peter, 'Thou hast the words of eternal life' (Jn 6[68]). '*We have seen*' that gospel wonderfully lived out in His life, death and resurrection. '*We have seen*' Him giving new life to sinners and outcasts, and have stood amazed at His mighty works of healing; we have watched Him as He met the hostility and schemings of His enemies, and as He strode to Jerusalem to die on the Cross. Yes, and '*we have seen*' Him die, and heard that last triumphant cry: 'It is finished.' Before He came to the Cross, and as '*we beheld*' Him (cf. John 1[14]), we knew that He was none other than the Messiah of God; and when He came back to us as the Risen Christ, and—strange fact—'*our hands handled*' Him (see Lk 24[39], Jn 20[27]), we knew that He was indeed the very Son of God. Yes, this is the evidence on which our faith is grounded; the evidence of men who, some sixty years ago, had first-hand experience of the life and person of the incarnate Son of God.

The modern preacher cannot claim, as John could, to have been an on-the-spot observer of the ministry of Jesus. But surely one of the major results of the intensive study of the Gospels in this century is that we can accept with a renewed confidence the reliability of the Gospel records and the apostolic interpretation of the life and person of Christ which they contain. But more; the human Jesus of Palestine is identical in character and purpose with the Exalted Christ, of whose presence and power *we* have intimate, first-hand experience today. Nor must we forget what Jesus said to Thomas: 'Blessed are they that have not *seen*, and yet have *believed*' (Jn 20[29]). By faith, in a spiritual rather than a physical sense, but with strong certainty, we can claim to hear and see and behold and touch the Contemporary Christ. This note of certainty, based on a personal experience of Christ which John shares with his readers and with the Christians of all centuries, rings throughout the Epistle and comes to tremendous climax in 5[18-21]. See *Note 27*, p. 124.

1[2]. '*And the life . . . the eternal life . . . was manifested*'. The truth that salvation means the gift of eternal life, that Christ Himself *is* the life and that He freely offers it to all, was the master theme of the teaching of Jesus, according to John's Gospel; and John has written this epistle that Christians may

'*know*' that they have this life, and on what conditions (5¹³).
In *Note 2* (p. 17), the teaching of Jesus on this vital subject, and
John's commentary on it, are summarized, and the preacher is
reminded that man today desperately needs this saving
message.

'*We bear witness and declare*'. A witness must first have been
an *eye*-witness. As in any court of law, he is called to '*declare*'
not what somebody else has told him, but what he has actually
heard and seen for himself. So, says John, the divine life has
been '*manifested*'—lived out in this world—and we have '*seen*'
it; to us, it is a matter of first-hand, not of second or third-
hand experience. But a witness is more than an eye-witness; he
'*declares*' what he has heard and seen to others. But, in the
New Testament anyhow, he is more than an impartial 're-
porter'; he '*declares*' what he has heard and seen so vividly
and with such conviction that his hearers feel that they were
really 'on the spot' when these things happened, and are moved
to share the convictions of the witness about them. It was
in this same sense that, on the evening before His death, Jesus
said to His disciples, 'Ye also *bear witness*, because ye have
been with me from the beginning' (Jn 15²⁷), and on Ascension
Hill said to them, 'Ye shall be my *witnesses* . . . unto the uttermost parts of the earth' (Acts 1⁸). And the apostles never forgot that challenge; see Acts 2²²⁻³⁶, 3¹³⁻¹⁸, 5³⁰⁻². This same
command came to Paul after his conversion ('Thou shalt
be a *witness* for him unto all men of what thou hast *seen*
and *heard*'; Acts 22¹⁵), and to the end of his life he bore
heroic witness to Christ out of his own experience (see Phil
1¹²⁻¹⁴).

So, when John wrote '*We bear witness and declare unto you*',
as when he made a similar 'aside' in his Gospel (Jn 3¹¹), he
was challenging his readers to bear their own witness to the
life and work of their divine Saviour in the face of a hostile,
pagan world; a challenge which was bravely answered during
the dread persecution of the Church in Asia Minor under
Emperor Domitian, a few years after this pastoral was written.

And we modern preachers, like John and his colleagues,
must respond to Christ's call to be His witnesses in our own
age. Our task is not to air our own opinions or give good advice
from the pulpit. Even less is it to convince our people that we
are brilliant preachers! As James Denney once said: 'You can't
in preaching produce at the same time an impression of your

own cleverness, and that Christ is wonderful.' Our task is to witness to the Christ of the gospel story and, out of our own first-hand experience, to convince our hearers that this Christ is the living Saviour of all men (see 2 Cor 4⁵). We must say, with Charles Wesley,

> *O let me commend my Saviour to you,*
> *I set to my seal that Jesus is true:*
> *Ye all may find favour who come at His call;*
> *O come to my Saviour! His grace is for all.* (*MHB* 311)

And we must present this challenge to our hearers. No true Christian can keep to himself his experience of the saving power of Christ. Imagine a doctor, who has discovered an infallible cure for cancer, refusing to share his knowledge with the whole world! The Christian who tries to keep Christ to himself, in order to concentrate on the cultivation of his own inner life, is more likely to lose both his Saviour and his soul. We must challenge our people to '*bear witness*', and to '*declare*' to their fellows what Christ has come to mean to them, through their personal intimacy with Him and their experience of His transforming power. When Dr Colin Roberts led the Christian Commando Campaigns in the cities of England in the early 1940s, he often quoted a barrister who said: 'When I have a bad case, I make a long speech; but when I know I have a good case, I call the witnesses.' So today, Christ calls His witnesses. Let them reply,

> *My heart is full of Christ and longs*
> *Its glorious matter to* declare. (*MHB* 270)

1³. Religion was once defined by A. N. Whitehead, the philosopher, as 'what a man does with his solitariness'. That is a very unsatisfactory definition of Christianity. Wesley was right, and in harmony with John, when he said: 'The Bible knows nothing about solitary religion.' One purpose of the witness of John and his associates to the historical facts on which the 'Gospel of Life' is based is '*that ye also* [i.e. as well as other Christians] *may have fellowship with us*'. The word '*fellowship*' is used by John only here and in **1⁶⁻⁷**, and does not appear in his Gospel; but the idea of fellowship in its deepest sense is prominent in his Gospel and, as we shall see, dominates the thought of this Epistle. The unity of the churches in the

Ephesus district had been broken by the mischievous exponents of the 'new theology' (see p. 4). In order to stop this drift into splinter-groups, and to re-establish that unity, John reminds his hearers that, if they repudiate the basic facts of Christianity, they disrupt the *'fellowship'* of the Church.

The Greek word *'koinonia'*, which is here translated *'fellowship'* or 'communion', means 'a sharing of something with someone' by 'partners' or 'joint-shareholders' (see Lk 5[10]). In the New Testament, this word (and words derived from it) sometimes refers to the sharing of money or goods; to the primitive Christian experiment in common ownership or 'communism' in Acts 2[44], 4[32]; to a 'contribution' (*'koinonia'*) to the Jerusalem Poor Fund in Romans 15[26], 2 Corinthians 9[13]; to a financial 'sharing' with Paul during his imprisonment in Philippians 4[13-15]; see also Romans 12[13], Galatians 6[6], Hebrews 13[16]. But *'fellowship'* in its deepest sense is based on the fact that the individual Christian, through self-commital to Christ, has *'fellowship'* with the Father, the Son and the Holy Spirit. That is what John means when he writes, *'yea, and our fellowship is with the Father, and with His Son Jesus Christ'*. The believer's communion with God is emphasized in Paul's letters (see *KG*, p. 83), in John 14-17 and throughout *1 John*. It is studied in detail in *Note 10*, p. 48.

The initial act of faith, in which a man makes his own encounter with Christ his Saviour, is an individual affair. But as soon as he becomes at-one with Christ, he becomes a 'sharer' in Christ with all other true Christians; at-one with them in the most intimate of all human fellowships. It is as you listen to and accept the Gospel of Life, says John, that you become one with Him who *is* the Life, who *is* the Gospel, and so you become one with us and with each other in your sharing of His divine presence and power. One by one you come to your Saviour, but as you come you *meet* together at His feet and, sharing His company, you journey together into newness of life; and how can you ever break away from each other, after that? Do you not share with each other the wonder of the gospel message when it is preached to you, and the challenge of His new commandment 'that ye love one another . . . even as I have loved you'? Do you not share together the thrill of the one true faith that is grounded on that gospel, through which the Christian can triumph over all the powers of evil? If you belong, each one of you, to the same Christ, you cannot cease to belong to each other. It follows that, in so far as you break away from the fellowship into little splinter-groups of individualists, you are repudiating your mutual sharing in the gospel, in the faith which is based on it, and in Christ who is the heart of it.

Is the life of the modern Church dominated by this sense of our unique *'fellowship'*? To say that the fellowship of many churches today is more like that of a religious club, and that it chiefly consists of friendly smiles, genial hand-shakes and a jolly gregariousness, is an exaggeration which contains an uncomfortable twinge of truth. We have certainly devalued the word. We announce from our pulpits the activities of the Men's Fellowship, the Women's Fellowship and the Youth Fellowship. We speak of the fellowship we enjoy as we work for the annual bazaar, or as we sit down to the Harvest Home Supper. Do we realize that the Church is not an institution to which is attached a number of local 'fellowships', but is itself *the* fellowship; the common fellowship of those who share with each other the very life of God Himself which is given to them through Jesus Christ?

But the *'fellowship'* of the early Christians was not merely a sense of unity; it was expressed in the observance of certain 'means of grace' through which their common partnership in Christ and the Faith was deepened and in which new dis-coveries were made of the 'unsearchable riches of Christ'; public worship, meetings for prayer, the sacrament of Holy Communion, and small gatherings in whose intimacy inquirers could be pointed to their Saviour and believers could be instructed in the Faith (see Mt 18[20]). The importance of this last form of fellowship needs stressing today. Addressing the Methodist Conference in 1766, Wesley said: 'What avails public preaching *alone*, though we could preach like angels? . . . We must instruct (our people) *from house to house*; till this is done, and that in good earnest, the Methodists will be little better than other people. . . . I study to speak as plain as I can; yet I frequently meet with those who have been my hearers many years, who know not whether Christ be God or man. . . . And how few are there that know the nature of repentance, faith, and holiness! Most of them have a sort of confidence that Christ will justify and save them, while the world has their hearts, and they live to themselves. And I have found by experience, that one of these has learned more from an hour's close discourse, than from ten years' public preaching.' Would not the modern preacher agree, out of his own experience? Dr Dale said that the Class Meeting was the most striking of the fruits of the Methodist Revival. It is good today that the Church as a whole, and not the Methodist Church only, is rediscovering the vital importance of this form of fellowship, into which we can welcome those who are groping their way towards Christ, and in which believers may seriously study the Bible and the essentials of the Faith, gain a deeper experience of Christ's saving power, and be encouraged in Christian living.

1[4], '*that our joy may be fulfilled*'. So read the best MSS; not 'your joy' as in *AV*. The phrase seems to be a deliberate reference to the words of Jesus on the evening before the Cross: 'that my joy may be in you, and that your joy may be fulfilled' (Jn 15[11]). Through all His trials and agonies, Jesus was essentially the Man of Joy, and the secret of His joy was His uninterrupted communion with God, His perfect trust in Him, and His sacrificial self-giving to the fulfilment of God's will. And, said Jesus to His disciples, if you unreservedly commit yourselves to me and my service, you will share my overflowing joy in the divine communion. This is the joy—'*our joy*'— which John and his colleagues experience; and their joy will be '*fulfilled*', filled full and overflowing, if they can lead others into this same joyous fellowship with Christ and with each other.

One of the striking qualities of the early Christians was their exuberant joy. It began when the apostles met the risen Lord in the Upper Room (Jn 20[20]) and it was communicated to every convert who joined their fellowship. Paul, for instance, was once a very able but rather dull young rabbi; but when he and Silas were clamped to the stocks in an underground dungeon in Philippi, they made the whole jail ring with the sound of their joyous hymns of praise. And Paul was again in jail when he wrote his letter to the Philippians, and in an even more perilous plight; but see how the note of joy runs through that letter (Phil 1[18], 2[16-18], 3[1], 4[1, 4, 10]). Think of Francis of Assisi and his merry troubadours, in a later age. Hear the words of John Wesley as he describes the Methodist in one of his first tracts (1739): 'He is therefore happy in God; yes, always happy.... Perfect love having cast out fear, he rejoices evermore.' Listen to Charles Wesley as he teaches us to sing,

> *In the heavenly Lamb*
> *Thrice happy I am,*
> *And my heart it doth dance at the sound of His name.*
>   (*MHB* 406)

But Dr Jacks has used the phrase 'the lost radiance of the Christian religion', and Walter Lippmann of America has written of 'grimly spiritual persons devoted to the worship of sonorous generalities'. By many people outside the Church the Christian today is regarded as a solemn, joyless person who gets no fun out of life and resents anybody else wanting to do so. Dorothy Sayers, in *Creed or Chaos*, compiled a series of questions about Christianity, and the answers to them which the average non-Christian might give. The series concluded as follows:

Q. What are the seven Christian virtues?
A. Respectability; childishness; mental timidity; dullness; sentimentality; censoriousness; and depression of spirits.
Q. Wilt thou be baptized in this faith?
A. No fear!

Dullness! Depression of spirits! What a contrast to the exultant joy, the infectious rapture, which glow from the life of the real Christian. The man whose fellowship with Christ has not made him joyous, the man who seems to practise the 'cult of miserableness', is a poor witness for his Saviour. We must recall our people to the secret of that invincible joy which persists through sorrow and hardship, through tribulation and tragedy, to the end. The Christian life is not a solemn and gloomy pilgrimage to death, but a gay and thrilling adventure into life, in company with Christ. This is the joyous life which we preachers want all men and women to share with us, '*that our joy may be fulfilled*' (see *KG*, p. 85).

NOTE 1. CHRISTIANITY IS BASED ON HISTORY

Christianity is not a system of *ideas* about God. The Christians to whom John was writing were living among 'pagans' whose highest forms of religion consisted of philosophical abstractions about the Deity which were the result of intellectual speculation. God was infinite, ineffable, omnipotent, and so on. Further, the heretics who had just left the Church were claiming to have a unique mystic experience by means of which they received secret information about the mystery of the Godhead; a 'gnosis' which could be expressed in the form of timeless, transcendent and discarnate truth. They disparaged that primitive interest in the facts of the gospel story which was felt by 'inferior' Christians who were only at the rudimentary stage of spiritual development. If their teaching had won the day, Christianity would have become a vague, mystical fellowship with a Spirit Christ who had nothing to do, or very little to do, with the Jesus of History. And even today there are writers who say: 'We have the contemporary Christ, and are not interested in what happened in Palestine long centuries ago. Whether the Gospels are historically reliable is a minor matter to us. Even if it were proved that the human Jesus had never lived, our Christianity, our Christian *ideas* about God, would still survive.'

John, however, does not begin his letter by saying: 'We think that we have found a satisfactory philosophy of religion, and that God must be like this and that.' He starts with the assumption that Christianity is not the result of men's search after God that 'they might feel after him, and find him' (Acts 17²⁷). On the contrary, it is based upon God's disclosure of Himself on the plane of human history in dramatic events of judgement and redemption; events which took place in time, but which were invested by God with an eternal significance; events whose contemporary meaning and timeless message were interpreted to men by those whom He inspired for this purpose—the prophets and the apostles (see Comment on 1¹⁻³).

John's assumption is true to the whole message of the Bible; to the Old Testament, with its record of God's choice of Israel as the medium of His self-revelation and of His mighty-saving acts which prepared the way for the supreme event of history; to the Gospels, with their record of God's unique and final disclosure of Himself in the birth, ministry, death, resurrection and exaltation of Jesus Christ, His own Son, when Augustus and Tiberius ruled in Rome and Pontius Pilate was procurator of Judea; to the 'Acts', with its description of the continuing work of Christ, through the Holy Spirit, in the life of the Early Church; and to the apostolic interpretation of the person and work of Christ in the epistles and the Apocalypse. These concrete, historic events of final and absolute significance—these mighty acts in which God visited His people that He might make Himself known to them and might redeem them—are the unshakable basis of the primitive faith (see the Apostles' Creed) and of our faith today. They are the substance of the primitive Christian preaching, and of our preaching today. We must insist that every professing Christian should be a serious student of the Bible, and especially of the New Testament. The believer who does not know the Jesus of History will always be very vague about the Christ of Experience.

NOTE 2. ETERNAL LIFE

Whatever else he is interested in, surely every man is interested in the life he is living and the life he would prefer to live. Then sooner or later—though, perhaps, not until tragedy shatters his apathy— he must face the question: 'Has life any real meaning or lasting significance?' Many who have faced that question have answered it with a decisive 'No', from Gautama Buddha in the fifth century B.C. to Thomas Hardy and Bertrand Russell in our own times. Indeed, some of our modern philosophers have gone even farther and invented a philosophy of 'Nihilism' or 'Meaninglessness'. Their creed is: 'Nothing is indestructible, nothing has eternal value, and so nothing is worth living for. Life has no more meaning than a nightmare.' It is no wonder that many of these thinkers are now rebelling against the terrible creed they have invented, and are seeking a spiritual answer to the question. But many of our contemporaries manage to get through most of their life without even looking at the question. They just jog along the roads of life, not caring whether they are highways or byroads. They are indifferent to the fact that every fork in a road calls for a serious decision. They ignore all sign-posts, because they are not going anywhere in particular; they have in view no destination which is *worth* reaching. Each morning they scurry into the clamour and bustle of modern business or industry; and each evening they scurry out of it, with no consciousness that their daily routine is getting them anywhere that really matters. They are just earning the means of paying their rent and the housekeeping bills, and keeping up their instalments on the TV and the washing-machine. And yet, though for the most part unconsciously, many of them are haunted with a sense of 'futility'—a popular word nowadays—and are no longer satisfied with the catch-phrase, 'I haven't a clue'. Are they becoming increasingly ready to listen to a preacher who can, with divine authority, answer the question: 'Has life any real meaning or lasting significance?'

Certainly, John offers them the answer, for the idea of 'life' dominates his writings. On page after page, he declares that the salvation which Christ offers to men is salvation *from* sin *into* eternal life. He wrote his Gospel 'that ye may believe . . . and that believing ye may have *life*' (Jn 20³¹). He wrote this epistle '*that ye may know that ye have eternal life*' (5¹³), and says that the theme of his letter is the Gospel of Life (1¹). Jesus Himself said that the purpose of His coming to earth was that men 'may have life, and may have it abundantly' (Jn 10¹⁰), and John says that God sent His Son '*that we might live through him*' (4⁹; cf. Jn 3¹⁶).

But what is this 'eternal life'? It certainly does not mean the endless duration of the life which men now live; the everlasting prolongation of the common humdrum of earthly life would terrify us rather than elate us. George Bernard Shaw used to say that, if our earthly span of years were increased from three-score-and-ten to three hundred, death would be looked on as a blessed relief. No, 'eternal' literally means 'belonging to an age'; and in the Jewish Apocalyptic writings, 'eternal life' meant—in contrast to the life of this Age—the life of the Age to Come; the life which all pious Jews hoped to enjoy when the Messiah had established the rule of God upon earth. So, to Jesus, to 'enter into the kingdom of God' and to 'possess eternal life' meant the same thing; cf Mark 9⁴³, ⁴⁵ with 9⁴⁷, and Mark 10¹⁷ with 10²³. 'Eternal life', therefore, is not mere duration of life; it is a new *quality* of life. Its secret is not in its length, but in its height and depth. It is the fuller, richer life that we live in fellowship with God, whereby we share the very life of God Himself.

But how can we possess this eternal life? We cannot earn it by holy endeavours and good works; that is what the rich young ruler wanted to do (Mk 10¹⁷). We can only receive it as a *gift* from God. So John says that '*God gave unto us eternal life*' (5¹¹; cf. Rom 6²³). And God '*gave*' us eternal life when He gave us His Son. Jesus meant that when He said, 'I am the life' (Jn 11²⁵, 14⁶), and 'I am the bread of life' (Jn 6³⁵, ⁴⁸). He was the very embodiment of that quality of life which is the life of God; if any man wants to find eternal life, he will find it in Christ. So, in 1¹⁻³, John talks of 'life', and then says that this life, this 'eternal life', has been heard, seen, manifested on earth; that is, in the person of Christ. In offering Himself to men, Christ offered them eternal life (see Jn 4¹⁴, 5²⁴, ⁴⁰, 6⁶³, ⁶⁸, 10²⁸, 11²⁵⁻⁶, etc.). So, John writes, '*God gave unto us eternal life, and this life is in his Son. He that hath the Son hath the life*' (5¹¹⁻¹²) and '*This is the promise which he* (Christ) *promised us, even the life eternal*' (2²⁵). In so far as we 'believe on' Jesus Christ, and unreservedly commit ourselves to Him in faith, and live the life of faith-union with Him, He imparts to us that eternal life which is the very essence of salvation (5¹³, Jn 3¹⁶; see also *Note 10*, p. 48). How cordially John would agree with the man who said: 'A day out of Christ is a day lost for ever.'

It follows that our experience of eternal life can begin *here and now*. Eternal life (like entering into the Kingdom of God) is both a *future* and a *present* experience; but in the Johannine writings, every reference to 'eternal life' (with the one exception of John 12²⁵) is to Christ's unique teaching that that life can begin *here and now*, in the midst of our mortality. Look at the words of Jesus in John's Gospel. The promise of John 4¹⁴, the '*hath* eternal life' of John 5²⁴, 6⁴⁷, ⁵⁴, and such words as those in John 6⁴⁰, 11²⁶, all speak of eternal life as a here-and-now experience. John's own comments in John 3¹⁵⁻¹⁶, ³⁶ make the same point. So also, in 3¹⁴, John says that we Christians '*know that we have passed out of death into life*'. Again, in 5¹²⁻¹³, '*hath the life*' and '*have eternal life*' refer to a present experience (see also Comment on 5²⁰). Yes, even now, through Christ, the believer can begin to live that fuller, richer life which is a sharing of the very life of God Himself; a new life which is the result of a New Birth (see *Note 15*, p. 77), and which will transform every part of his present earthly existence, and give it a new dimension. Are we and our people living this superhuman life? Can we say: 'Now we know what Jesus meant when He said "more abundantly". It has already begun for us! Full, exuberant, dynamic life! Eternal Life!'? And are other people startled by the divine quality of it? And, as we continue to live 'in Christ', do we experience more and more of the transforming power of it? The trouble is that so many middle-aged Christians tend to settle down spiritually. Instead of wanting more life, they begin to want less. They no longer want to think more, to feel more, to fit themselves for larger responsibilities and mightier tasks. Christ offers them eternal life in increasing measure, and they murmur, 'Enough, Lord! Enough!'

We have seen that 'eternal', when applied to 'life', does not mean mere endlessness; but, if eternal life is a quality of life which the believer shares with God through Christ, then by its very nature it must be everlasting. It cannot end; it defies physical death (3¹⁴) and goes on towards its consummation in the life hereafter. But what John stresses is that, right here and now, we can enjoy a real foretaste of the final blessedness of the heavenly life.

> *Thou of life the fountain art,*
> *Freely let me take of Thee,*
> *Spring Thou up within my heart,*
> *Rise to all eternity.* (*MHB* 110)

(A) 1⁵-2²⁸. THE CHRISTIAN LIFE IS A LIFE OF FELLOWSHIP WITH GOD.

(a) 1⁵-2⁶. The Test of Right Living

In this section, John begins his attack on the heretical teachers who say that the primitive gospel of the apostles is too elementary for advanced Christians like themselves, and who claim to have a unique spiritual experience because of their superior enlightenment (see p. 16). He quotes the claims they make; '*We have fellowship with him*' (1⁶); '*We have no sin*' (1⁸); '*We have not sinned*' (1¹⁰); '*I know him*' (2⁴); '*I abide in him*' (2⁶)— and then shows that their actual behaviour gives the lie to these boasts. In doing so, he uses the contrasting opposites of light and darkness, truth and falsehood, righteousness and sin which appear so often in his Gospel.

1⁵⁻⁷. Summary: *God is pure light. It follows that we must aim at living a life of radiant goodness, freed by Christ from all sin. Only so can we have unbroken fellowship with God and with each other.*

1⁵. The question which dominates **1⁵-2²⁸**—'Are you living a life of fellowship with God?'—arises from **1³**. But, that his readers may understand what such fellowship implies, John gives a description of the nature of God; a description which the heretics themselves would accept, though they fail to grasp the depth of its meaning and its practical implications. '*God is light.*' This is not what John has discovered for himself by intensive thought; it is a '*message*' which he and his associates ('*we*') have '*heard*' from Christ Himself (see **1¹⁻³**) and which they now '*announce*'. This description of God as '*light*' calls for detailed study; see *Note 3*, p. 23.

In the rest of this section (**1⁶-2⁶**), '*we*' means 'any professing Christian'.

1⁶⁻⁷ᵃ. If the nature of God is '*light*'—radiant goodness—and if the Christian would '*have fellowship with him*' (**1⁶**), he must '*walk* [=live and behave] *in the light, as he* [God] *is in the light*' (**1⁷ᵃ**). That means that he must commit himself so completely to Christ that, partaking of His nature, he may live out day by day that life of splendour which the human Jesus lived, and which is the very life of God Himself. So, when Jesus said, 'Ye are the light of the world', He meant that what shines from the life of the Christian is not his own light; it is God's light imparted to him through union with Christ (Mt 5¹⁴⁻¹⁶). In so far as our life is free from all darkness of sin, and aglow with the light of radiant goodness, we become sons of light Jn (12³⁶) and can truly claim to have fellowship with God, for we can meet THE TEST OF RIGHT CONDUCT. But more; sharing together this divine fellowship, '*we have fellowship one with another* (**1⁷ᵃ**; see comment on **1³**). Herein is the secret of the unity of the Church.

But in **1⁶** John is quoting one of the boasts of the heretics: '*We have fellowship with him.*' They make this claim, and yet their behaviour does not glow with the light that is divine. On the contrary, they '*walk in the darkness*'; they live and act in the realm of moral evil. As we have seen (p. 5), the heretics had adopted from the Gnostics a doctrine of salvation which over-stressed the importance of the intellect and emotion, and minimized the importance of right behaviour. For the moment, John does not give the details of the misbehaviour which resulted from their ethical indifference; he will do so in $1^{8, 10}, 2^{4, 9-11}, 3^{10, 15, 17}, 4^{8}$. Here he is content to say that their behaviour within the Church and among their brethren shows that their boast is a plain '*lie*'. They signally fail to meet the test of right conduct. For '*do not the truth*', see *Note 4*, p. 25. So, because they are out of fellowship with God, they are disrupting the fellowship of believers.

Throughout this letter, as we shall see, John stresses the danger of a divorce between religious experience and moral conduct. In the second century, when the heresy which John attacked became much more widespread, this divorce became so serious that the moral standards of many Christians were lower than those of their pagan neighbours, and their misconduct brought great discredit upon the Church and its faith. In no century has the Church been free from this error; an error which has often weakened its witness to the world. John Wesley encountered a type of mysticism which encouraged indifference to moral conduct and the disciplines of the Christian life, and dealt faithfully with it. We must heed his warning. We sing Thomas Binney's words,

> *Eternal Light! Eternal Light!*
> *How pure the soul must be,*
> *When, placed within Thy searching sight,*
> *It shrinks not, but, with calm delight,*
> *Can live, and look on Thee! (MHB 544)*

but we may unconsciously refuse to allow that 'searching sight' to expose our secret sins and shatter into fragments our 'calm delight'. We must remind ourselves that an exalted feeling of communion with God which is not matched with a life of splendid living is an illusion.

1^{7b}. Unchristian behaviour has disrupted the fellowship; but, says John, this need not be so, for '*the blood of Jesus . . . cleanseth us from all sin*'. Churchgoers are dangerously familiar with this great text. We sing with enthusiasm such lines as—

> *His blood can make the foulest clean,*
> *His blood availed for me. (MHB 1)—*

c

but how many of us understand the meaning of the words?

(*a*) '*the blood of Jesus*'. In the Jewish sacrificial system the blood of the victim was regarded as its *life* ('The blood is the life', Deut 12[23]; cf. 2 Sam 23[17]). On the night before the Cross Jesus gave wine to His disciples and said: 'This is my blood . . . which is *shed for* many' (Mk 14[24]; see *CLM*, pp. 101, 104-5). The wine was the symbol of His final sacrifice when, as the Representative of all sinners, He would lay down His life to make it possible for penitents to be reconciled to God. This conception of '*the blood of Jesus*' as *shed* to make expiation for sin appears in **2[2]** (see comment), though the word 'blood' is not mentioned.

In his Gospel, however, John does not stress Christ's death as an act of expiation. In John 13, he omits the institution of the sacrament and the words of Mark 14[24]. Instead, in John 6[51b-7], he inserts words which were perhaps spoken by Jesus in the Upper Room after He had given the bread and wine to the disciples; 'He that . . . drinketh my blood hath eternal life . . . abideth in me' (Jn 6[54, 56]). This does not contradict the thought of Mark 14[24], but it gives a fuller meaning to 'my blood'. It is not only the blood *shed for* men—that was not the end of His self-giving, but the beginning. It is also the blood *offered to* men. Jesus looked towards the Cross, and beyond it, to an endless ministry in which the Exalted Christ would offer His 'blood'—Himself, with all His life-giving power—to all who would receive it. And that is what John means by '*the blood of Jesus*' in **1[7]**.

(*b*) '*cleanseth us from all sin*'; or rather, since the tense is present-continuous, 'goes on cleansing us'. We often sing—

> *Be of sin the double cure,*
> *Cleanse me from its guilt and power*. (*MHB* 498)—

and sometimes in the New Testament we find the idea of cleansing from *guilt*. But generally 'cleanse' is used of liberation from the *power* of sin. Just as Jesus cleansed the leper by freeing him from his dreadful disease (Mk 1[40-4]), so He sought to cleanse the disciples from every unworthy thought and ambition, and in the Upper Room was able to say, 'Ye are clean'—though, remembering Judas, He had to add 'but not all' (Jn 13[10]; cf. 15[2-3]). Here, as also in Matthew 5[8], Jesus was speaking of cleansing from the *power* of sin. We are sure that '*cleanseth*' has this meaning in **1[7b]** when we turn to **1[9]**, where

John makes a clear distinction between *'forgive us our sins'* (that is, free us from the guilt of them) and *'cleanse us from all unrighteousness'* (that is, liberate us from the power of sin). On the significance of *'all'* in **1^{7b}** and **1⁹**, see *Note 5*, p. 35.

To sum up; in **1^{7b}** John says that Christ's continuous giving of Himself to us has a tremendous moral and spiritual effect; it does for us and in us what we cannot do by our own effort; it delivers us more and more from the servitude of sin and transforms us, however slowly, from sinners into true disciples (cf. Rev 7¹⁴).

> *He breaks the power of cancelled sin,*
>   *He sets the prisoner free;*
> *His blood can make the foulest clean,*
>   *His blood availed for me.* (*MHB* 1)—

though perhaps 'availed' should be 'avails', if Charles Wesley was referring to **1^{7b}**.

NOTE 3. GOD IS LIGHT

Ever since the far-off ages when the Sun was worshipped as the benefactor of the human race, God has been associated with *light*. The Persians thought of the age-long conflict between good and evil in terms of light and darkness. Plato said that the ultimate reality is light, and the Mystery religions used the same symbolism. One of the basic assumptions of the Gnosticism of John's day (see p. 5) was that *'God is light'*, and that only light can give salvation. So John knew that the phrase, *'God is light'*, would 'ring a bell' in the minds of his pagan contemporaries, though what he meant by it was not what the Gnostics meant by it. When Jesus said 'I am the light', and when John said *'God is light'*, the background of their thought was the Old Testament.

In the Old Testament, 'light' is often used of those saving activities of God through which He revealed Himself to man. Often, it is the symbol of the revelation of God's nature (Ps 4⁶, 27¹, 43³) and of His will for men (Ps 119¹⁰⁵, Prov 6²³). It is also the symbol of God's salvation and the joy and security it brings to men (Ps 118²⁷, Isa 60¹, Mic 7⁸). But only in fitful gleams did the light of God's nature shine into the Hebrew mind. The basic Old Testament conception is that the true nature of God is still shrouded in mystery; that 'clouds and darkness are round about him' (Ps 97²; cf. Ex 20²¹, Deut 4¹¹, 2 Sam 22¹⁰). Not until the final Age of God would God's light shine upon men in all its glory (Isa 60¹⁹, Zech 14⁶⁻⁷).

When Jesus said that the only thing to do with a lighted lamp is to put it 'on a stand, that they which enter in may see the light' (Lk 8¹⁶),

He stressed the fact that light, by its very nature, cannot be self-contained; it must fulfil its proper function; it must shine; it must communicate itself to the outside world. So, when John says 'God is light', he means that God, by His very nature, must reveal Himself to mankind. The Gnostics contended that, for the vast majority of men, the God of light is hidden in mystery, and that He only reveals Himself to a select few who are specially 'enlightened'. John flatly contradicts that heresy; God communicates Himself to *all* who will receive the light of His self-revelation (see also *Note 8*, p. 43). When we sing

> *Immortal, invisible, God only wise,*
> *In light inaccessible hid from our eyes*   (*MHB* 34)

we are stating the truth, but not the whole truth. But, as we see in *Note 14*, p. 68, God can perfectly reveal Himself only through an incarnation, and this He has done in the person of Jesus Christ, His Son. In Him, the Age to Come (see above) has arrived. So, when Jesus was born in Bethlehem, 'there was the true light, even the light which lighteth every man, coming into the world' (Jn 1^9). So Jesus could say 'I am the light of the world' (Jn 8^{12}, 9^5), and in the last week of His earthly life could say, 'While ye have the light, believe on the light' (Jn 12^{35}). Although John said *This is the message which we have heard from him* (Christ) . . . *that God is light'* (1^5), as far as we know, Jesus did not actually use those words; but, by all that He Himself was and said and did, He declared that God is a God of light who reveals Himself to men in His Son. There is still mystery in our thought of God, but—and here we part company with the Agnostics—He who is the 'light of the world' has told us all that we mortal men will ever need to know about the character of God.

If 'light' symbolizes the radiant goodness of God, its opposite, 'darkness', stands for moral evil, and John stresses this contrast in 1^{5-7}, 2^{8-11}, Jn 1^5, 3^{19}, 8^{12}, $12^{35, 46}$ (cf. Col 1^{12-13}, Eph 6^{12}). John therefore seems to be stating the obvious when, in 1^5, he adds *'and in him is no darkness at all'*. How can there be moral imperfection in the being of God? But, as G. G. Findlay suggested (*GGF*, pp. 96-7), most of John's readers were converts from the old pagan religions of Asia Minor, and the gods they had once worshipped were thought of as possessing mixed natures, like our own but on a larger scale. They could cheat and lie, they could give way to gross passions, they could be spiteful and vicious in their dealings with men, and could quarrel among themselves! These converts must get rid of the last traces of such a conception of God. They must be reminded of that truth which came to them with the force of an amazing revelation when they first believed on Christ, that God is radiant goodness, nothing but radiant goodness; that in Him there is *'no darkness at all'*. But many people today—even many devout Christians—discredit God with all sorts of motives, passions and purposes which are common to the natural man. To ultra-sensitive people, God is a harsh Judge; to easy-going people, a genial, doting Parent. Some think of Him as a capricious and rather touchy Deity; others, as a Sectarian God who is specially fond of Anglicans or Methodists or Plymouth Brethren. To some, He is a 'Don't do this' God whose will is always expressed in a formidable list of irksome prohibitions; to others, He is an untrustworthy God who so often 'lets us down' just when we most need His help; to others, He is a God who is so busy looking after this infinite universe that He cannot be particularly interested in a spastic baby or a blind Old Age Pensioner—and so on. Again and again we must stress the fact that '*in him is no darkness at all*'.

For what John means by walking 'in the light' and 'in the darkness', see comment on **1**[6-7a].

NOTE 4. THE TRUTH

The Greek noun which is always translated 'truth' in *EVV* is one of the key-words of John. In ordinary usage, it meant what it usually means to us today; a statement which corresponds to fact, in contrast to one which is false. John uses the word in this sense in **4**[6], where '*truth*' is contrasted with '*error*'.

But the word was also used, in a religious and philosophical sense, to mean *reality* as opposed to mere *appearance* or *phantasy*; that which is real as opposed to what is unreal. Paul often used the word in this sense, and this is what John nearly always means by '*the truth*'. In his mind it stands for the unchanging, ultimate Reality, God as He really is—and for knowledge of that divine Reality as it has been given to men. When Jesus spoke of 'the one true God' (Jn 17[3]) and when John wrote '*This is the one true God*' (**5**[20]) by 'true' they meant 'real'. So to John '*the truth*' means that whole revelation of God as He really is, in all His gracious nature and activity, which has been given to us by Christ; a revelation which has also disclosed what man is really meant to be, how real sin is, and what real life is like. That is what John meant when he said that Christ was 'full of truth' (Jn 1[14]), that 'truth came by Jesus Christ' (Jn 1[17]) and that Christ was '*the true light*' (**2**[8]; cf Jn 1[9], 6[32], 15[1]). And that was what Jesus Himself meant when He said 'I am the truth' (Jn 14[6]). He came to reveal what God is really like; but not merely in words, definitions, and formulae. He lived out that reality in His own life; He *was* what God is really like; He was Reality incarnate. So, when Pilate, voicing the disillusionment of his age (and of ours) in its quest for reality, asked 'What is truth?' (Jn 18[38]), Reality itself stood before him. It is when we know and experience Christ that we know and experience God as He really is. Then we are no longer puzzled seekers, peering into the mystery of reality and reaching up towards God with reverent guesses. This is our message to the man of today who has come to doubt whether life has any meaning at all; whether there *is* any ultimate Reality.

The revelation which Jesus gave could not be grasped at once by His earthly disciples, but Jesus promised to come back into the life of believers in the person of His *alter ego*, the 'Spirit of truth' (Jn 14^{17}, 15^{26}), who would guide them 'into all the truth' (Jn 16^{13}, cf. 14^{26}). And, writes John, the Spirit of Truth can do this because '*the Spirit is the truth*' (5^7); He is the *alter ego* of Him who said 'I am the truth'. And this work the Spirit of Reality continues in us to this day.

It follows that, when John says that '*the truth is not in us*' (1^8; see also 2^4), he means that the right understanding of Christ's revelation of God has not come home to us; that Christ, who *is* Reality, is not fully dwelling in us; that we are therefore living in a world of unreality, phantasy, make-belief. On the other hand, when John says that his readers '*know the truth*' (2^{21}, 2 Jn 1; cf. Jn 8^{32}), he means that they have committed themselves to Christ who is the Truth, the revelation of eternal Reality; that, therefore, they '*know*' God as He really is, in the light of His searching scrutiny they '*know*' themselves as they really are, and they '*know*' what God requires them to be and the life He requires them to live. (On 'knowing God', see *Note 8*, p. 43.) '*We are of the truth*' (3^{19}) means 'We have committed ourselves to Christ, who is the Truth, and He has made us what we are'.

In 1^6, John says '*we do not the truth*' (cf Jn 3^{21}). Christ's revelation of the real will and nature of God is not merely something to be accepted by the mind; it must be lived out in conduct which is inspired by that revelation. To '*do the truth*' means to '*know the truth*' (see above), and then, in fellowship with Christ, to put it into practice. Quite simply, it means to live out your faith as a Christian. This, John says in 1^6, the heretics are failing to do—but he speaks to us, too. How difficult it is to put our highest convictions into daily practice.

1^8–2^2. **Summary:** *But the man who says 'I am not a sinner' deceives himself and rejects the gospel. We must confess the sin that still remains in us, that we may be forgiven; and we can be forgiven because of what Christ has done and is doing for us.*

1^8. At first sight, 1^8 and 1^{10} seem to be flatly contradicted by 3^9, '*Whosoever is begotten of God doeth no sin . . . he cannot sin*', and also by 3^6, 5^{18}. John's conception of sin, and his treatment of sin in believers, must be studied in detail. See *Note 5*, p. 35, and *Note 6*, p. 36, which the preacher is advised to read before he deals with any of the above-mentioned texts.

'*we have no sin*'. Again, John quotes one of the boasts of the heretics. The phrase means: 'Sin, that bias to unbelief and egoism which perverts a man's whole personality, is no longer at work within us.' The heretics claimed that, because of their special 'enlightenment', they had been given an entirely *new nature* which was so superior to that of the ordinary Christian that they were already sinless people. We see, in *Note 6*, that this boast was based on a quite inadequate conception of sin. In actual fact, as we see when we study 2^{9-11}, 3^{10-11}, $^{14-15}$, 4^{20}, their complete lack of love for their 'inferior' brethren exposed them as flagrant sinners.

'*we deceive ourselves*'. John's blunt warning against self-deception was not meant for the heretics only; it was directed to all his readers—and to us. One of Christ's major problems is the declared Christian who prevents his Saviour from carrying on His saving work within him by surrounding himself with a high fence of self-deception and dishonesty. He may be an over-confident young convert, who glories in the fact that he is now a 'saved man' and that he has been 'washed in the blood of the Lamb' from every taint of sin; and yet pride and self-will are still subtly and dangerously at work within him. But he is more likely to be a Christian who has been professing the Christian faith for twenty or thirty years, who is sure that he is a good average Christian, and who obstinately rejects the preacher's challenge to self-examination. We all know the middle-aged man who refuses to be medically examined because he is afraid that something seriously wrong may be discovered. Many a middle-aged Christian is as foolishly reluctant to allow God's probe to touch that sore spot in his soul where sin is still doing its dread work. Rather than do so, he will habitually deceive himself.

This face-saving technique takes many forms. *Euphemism*, for instance, is one of them; the craft of finding nice names for nasty activities. Other people steal; he only scrounges or 'wins' things. Others cheat; he is just 'canny'. Others may be cowardly; he is only 'discreet'. Others are rude; he is 'frank' and 'honest'. Touchiness when he is criticized is 'sensitiveness'; the flare-up of his temper when he is thwarted is 'righteous indignation'; and so on. *Rationalizing* is another method of self-deception; the unconscious tendency to find good reasons for doing evil things. In the Upper Room, when Jesus told the Twelve that one of them would betray Him, they 'looked one on another, doubting of whom he spake' (Jn 13²²), and one by one they asked Him, 'Lord, it isn't I, is it?'—the literal translation of Mark 14¹⁹. Matthew tells us that even Judas asked it (Mt 26²⁵). He was about to betray Jesus, but he had found a good reason for this foul deed. 'Betray'? No, he was really forcing Jesus's hand, so that here and now He would declare His messiahship and mount the throne of the world. In some such way, perhaps, Judas rationalized his sin, deceiving himself. How easy it is to act under the impulse of some undisciplined ambition, and then find respectable reasons for doing so. Caiaphas found a good reason for crucifying Jesus (Jn 11⁵⁰) and doubtless felt quite comfortable when he said his prayers on Good Friday evening!

Yes, it was respectable, religious people who were chiefly responsible for crucifying the world's Saviour; and the sin that moved them to this dreadful purpose still survives in us today. We are all *there* when they crucify our Lord.

'*the truth is not in us*'. See *Note 4*, p. 25.

1⁹. '*If we confess our sins*'. Confession of sins is mentioned only five times in the New Testament. In Mark 1⁵ = Matthew 3⁶ it is made to the Baptist, in Acts 19¹⁸ to Paul, and in James 5¹⁶ 'one to another'. Nowhere is there any suggestion of confession to a *priest*. Always, as in **1⁹**, the confession is really to *God*; cf. 'I will confess my transgressions unto the Lord' (Ps 32⁵). Many people today 'confess' to their psychoanalyst, who dissolves their sin into complexes and neuroses, and perhaps tells them not to worry about it; God's name may not even be mentioned. On the other hand, to confess to a sympathetic Christian friend, whether minister or lay man or woman, may help a sinner to make an honest confession to God.

'*our sins*'. It is significant that John here moves from 'sin' to '*sins*'; the thoughts, words and deeds in which sin expresses itself. Confession must begin with particular sins, rather than with general sinfulness. Many a man will glibly confess that he is a 'miserable sinner', but he will be deeply offended if anyone suggests that he is a liar or a scandal-monger, that he is sensual, jealous or covetous. He is more ready to confess the sins of the person in the next pew. But the sinner must do more than confess his '*sins*', what he has *done*; he must then confess his 'sin', what he *has been* and *is*; that is full confession.

Confession includes discovery, penitence and repudiation. The sinner acknowledges his sins to himself, no longer excusing himself but admitting his responsibility (Ps 51³). Then, in the presence of God, he repents of his sins and pledges himself to do them no more (Ps 51⁴). He owns and disowns both them and himself who did them. This is both a painful experience and a blessed relief. Now he can look Christ in the face and say: 'At last, Lord, I think about myself as *you* think about me.' He no longer averts his eyes as he passes the Cross; he looks at it and cries—

> *Two wonders I confess—*
> *The wonders of redeeming love,*
> *And my own worthlessness.* (*MHB* 197)

God '*is faithful*' to Himself 'whose property is always to have mercy'. He is never capricious or inconsistent. He can always, therefore, be relied upon to keep His promise—so often given— that the penitent sinner shall be forgiven. In your Concordance, look up '*faithful*' (especially noting 2 Timothy 2¹³) and '*forgive*' and its cognate words.

'*and righteous*'. Does that sound cold and rigid and unrelenting, and the reverse of merciful? Such a misconception has wrecked many a 'theory' of the atonement. To the Greeks, the righteousness of God was a quality of His character, and most Christians so think of it. But to the Jews, God's righteousness was not only an attribute; it was an *activity*. In the Old Testament, this activity was first thought of as the result of God's will to put His people Israel 'in the right'; to vindicate them, and save them from their oppressors (e.g. Judg 5¹¹). Later, a deeper meaning was given to God's righteousness; it was His mighty purpose to save His people from the slavery of *sin*, and through them to draw the whole world to Himself and into His kingdom. So, in Isaiah 51⁵, Yahweh says, 'My righteousness is near, my salvation is gone forth', and it is obvious that His righteousness and His salvation are one and the same activity (see S. C. Thexton on Isaiah 51⁵ in *EPC*).

In the Gospels, Jesus speaks of the righteousness of God only in Matthew 6³³ and John 17²⁵; but John and Paul, His interpreters, make it plain that, while 'righteousness' and 'salvation' are still identical terms, Jesus has transformed their meaning in one important respect. In the Old Testament, as we see in Isaiah 51⁵⁻⁷, God is thought of as vindicating those who are *already righteous*. If the Hebrews would experience the saving activity of Yahweh, they must first forsake all wicked ways and become righteous. In the New Testament, the righteousness of God, His saving activity, consists in the putting in the right, the declaring righteous, the 'justification', the forgiving of those who in fact are *not* righteous, but who are as yet only *penitent sinners*. So, says John, God is '*righteous*' to forgive the man who confesses his sins (see further, C. H. Dodd on Romans 1¹⁷ in *Moffatt Commentary*, *KG*, pp. 29-31).

'*to cleanse*'; see comment on 1⁷ᵇ.

'un*righteousness*' stands for man's wrongdoing against his fellow man.

1¹⁰. '*we have not sinned*'. John quotes another boast of the heretics, which goes even farther than the '*we have no sin*' of 1⁸. They claim, not only that *sin* no longer survives in them, but that, since their conversion (their 'enlightenment') they have never committed a solitary *act* of sin. They seem to have argued that 'if the enlightened do things which in other men would be counted sinful, they are not sinners. Their mystical communion with God in itself removes them from the category of sinful men' (*CHD*, pp. 21-2). The point is that they were committing sins—flagrant sins of pride and lovelessness—but that, when charged with them, they cried 'Not guilty!' They stared each individual sin in the face and said: 'That was not sin; nor that; nor that.'

It is very doubtful if any modern Christian would look back over his life since his conversion, and boast 'I have not sinned'; but most of us, when we remember the actual sins of the past week, are inclined to ease our conscience by pointing to the more glaring of them and saying: 'That was not sin; nor that; nor that!' If other people did that sort of thing, they would be sinning; but our sins are not really 'sins' at all. 'Desiring to justify himself' (Lk 10²⁹); we all do it. Conscience says, 'That was a sin'; and at once, with one touch of the button, all the defence-mechanism of self-justification is put into operation. Sometimes we say: 'I was *not myself* when I did it, so it wasn't a "sin". I didn't do it; it sort of "happened"!' Sometimes we push the blame on to *circumstances*. 'Yes, I lost my temper at the Trustees Meeting, but my gastric ulcer had just flared up.' Or: 'If you worked in the office I work in, you'd know how impossible it is to refuse to share a sweepstake or a sherry party.' At other times we shift the blame on to the shoulders of *other people*; a face-saving device which originated in the Garden of Eden. Before he 'came to himself' and cried 'I have sinned', the Prodigal Son probably blamed everybody but himself for his past misbehaviour. If his father hadn't been so strict, if his mother hadn't been so fussy, if his elder brother hadn't been such a cad; and so on. So often, other people are to blame. 'Yes, I quarrelled with my wife last night, but nobody who knows how infuriating my good woman can be would dream of blaming me.' And, of course, we can always blame *the Devil*. 'The temptation was overwhelming; all the odds were against me and my downfall was inevitable. Even God would admit that, and not chalk it up as a "sin".'

'*we make him a liar*'. When we '*deceive ourselves*' (1^8), we are largely acting unconsciously; but when we say that '*we have not sinned*', our argument is conscious, deliberate and defiant. It is sheer insolence. When God says, through our conscience, 'That was a sin', and we stare back defiantly and cry, 'It was not', we are calling God '*a liar*'. That is John's blunt reply. Either *you* are a liar, or *God* is!

'*his word is not in us*'. God's whole scheme of salvation assumes that all men are sinners, and that this is true, though to a lesser degree, even after they have been 'born from above'. It assumes, therefore, that the best of Christians commit occasional acts of sin (See *Note 6*), that they must still pray daily, 'Forgive us our trespasses', and that they still need the saving work which Christ will continue to do for them and in them. But to say '*we have not sinned*' is not only to call God '*a liar*'; it is also to say that we no longer need the saving work of Christ. This is a blunt rejection of God's '*word*' to us, the message of the gospel.

2^1. '*My little children*'. See comment on 2^{12-14}.

'*that ye may not sin*'. John has insisted that his readers must face the hard fact that, though believers, they are still sinners who are liable to sin (see *Note 6*, p. 36). Now he tells them that his real purpose in saying this is not to discourage them, but to assure them that Christ can deal with that sin, and the occasional sins they commit, until He has perfected them in love.

'*Advocate*'. The English form of the Greek word is 'Paraclete'.

Only John uses it. It literally meant 'One who is called in' to give help, and Jesus used it in this general sense in John 14[16], [26], 15[26]. But in a more special sense, it meant 'One who is called in' to assist a person in a court of law, either by giving evidence for him, or by pleading his case as his '*Advocate*'. There is no doubt that the word means '*Advocate*' in 2[1], as also in John 16[7-8]. In John 14-16, Jesus speaks of the Paraclete, or the Spirit, as His *alter ego*, His Other-Self. There is a *theological* distinction between the Son and the Holy Spirit, but both John and Paul write as if there is no difference in *experience* between the Spirit and the Indwelling Christ. (For fuller discussion, see *Note 20*, p. 96.) So, in John 16[7-8], Christ's Other-Self is our '*Advocate*' on earth, and in this case He is the Counsel for the prosecution; He will convict (i.e. cross-examine in order to prove guilty) unbelieving humanity. In 2[1], the Exalted Christ is our '*Advocate*' on high, and in this case He is the Counsel for the defence, the sinner being the defendant at the Judgement Seat of God and Satan being the accuser (cf. Rom 8[26-7], [34], Heb 7[25], 9[24]).

When a Christian commits a sin, and knows that it is a sin, his conscience drives him into the presence of God with a cry of 'Guilty!' and a plea for forgiveness—and by the side of God stands Christ, his '*Advocate*'. But why does he need an Advocate? To wheedle God into being gracious? No! To plead that there are extenuating circumstances, as if God does not understand how fierce temptation can be? No! Is it that he is not fit to plead his own cause? But before we answer that question, we must turn to the next verse, for John closely links together the fact that Christ is our '*Advocate*' with the fact that He is

2[2]. '*the propitiation for our sins*'. Nowhere in his Gospel does John refer to the sacrificial aspect of the life and death of Christ as an expiation for sin. This doctrine was based on such words of Jesus as those recorded in Mark 14[24] (see comment on 1[7b]), and it was prominent in the letters of Paul (see Rom 3[25], 5[9], Eph 1[7], 2[13], 5[2], Col 1[20]). But in this epistle John writes, 'Ye *know* that he was manifested to take away sins' (3[5]), and so seems to take it for granted that his readers are familiar with the Pauline doctrine. He does, however, make clear reference to the sacrificial theory in 2[2] and 4[10], where he uses the word '*propitiation*' (as Paul does in Romans 3[25]), though he does not actually refer to the 'blood' of Christ. The Greek noun translated '*propitiation*' comes from a verb which, in pagan writings, had two meanings. (i) It commonly meant to 'placate' or 'appease' an offended person or god; and 'to propitiate' still has that meaning in English. But nowhere in the New Testament is God an angry God who must be placated, and '*propitiation*' cannot have this meaning in 2^2, 4^{10}, and Romans 3^{25}, for in all three verses it is God Himself who provides the propitiation. (ii) It also meant 'to expiate a sin'; to do something—generally to make a sacrifice—by means of which the guilt of sin would be removed and the sinner could be forgiven. It is in this sense that John and Paul used the word '*propitiation*'. It is better translated 'expiation'. Even more simply, 2^2 could be paraphrased: 'He is the means by which our sins are forgiven.'

In what sense was Christ an expiation for men's sins? In His whole life, and supremely in His death, He offered to God, as the Representative of a world of sinners, what sinners must offer to the God of holy love before He can forgive them—and what they *could not* offer, just because of their indwelling sin. And what they could not offer, and what Christ offered on their behalf, was (i) a perfect obedience to the whole will of God, (ii) a perfect submission to God's judgement on their sin, and (iii) a perfect penitence for their sins (see V. Taylor, *Jesus and His Sacrifice*, pp. 307-12). But how does what Christ offered make it possible for God to forgive *us*, today, without condoning our sins? Perhaps we may begin to answer that question, if we return to 2^1 and the idea that Christ is our Advocate.

2^1. '*Advocate*'. The reconciling work of Christ's was not confined to the three years of His earthly ministry; it is a continuing work which will go on as long as men continue to sin. What *then* He offered on behalf of sinners, He offers always. At the heart of the Godhead is One who is still crucified by the sins of men, and who bears them in His heart that they may be forgiven. The Christian who has sinned approaches God with a plea for forgiveness, and what happens? Putting it very crudely—and that's inevitable—something like this. The penitent finds that there is no need for him to plead his own case, for there, by the Father's side, stands his '*Advocate, Jesus Christ the righteous*'. And the Advocate says to the Father, 'Father, this man has sinned again; but he is still Mine. In faith and love, he has committed himself to Me, and identified himself with Me and (as far as he can) with what I offer on his behalf; a perfect obedience, a perfect submission, a perfect penitence. The sin that remains in him still dulls his understanding, blunts his conscience, weakens his will; but as he continues to live in deepening fellowship with Me, he will be able to offer more and more perfectly what I now offer on his behalf.' And, because the sinner is 'in Christ', the Father is able to treat him, in advance as it were, as if he were a perfect son. The assurance of forgiveness is given.

'*Jesus Christ the righteous*'. He is '*righteous*' in the sense that God is righteous; see comment on 1⁹. Here, however, John uses the word in the sense of quality of character, as well as saving energy. Because Christ is the Perfect One, what He offers on our behalf is a perfect offering (cf. Heb 7²⁶).

2². '*the whole world*'. For what John means by '*the world*', see *Note 7*, p. 38. Here he stresses the fact that God's Plan of Salvation is not 'Operation Select', but 'Operation Humanity' —to quote Gordon Rupp. Unlike the heretics, he has no sympathy with that conception of a limited salvation which, centuries later, was expressed in its extreme form by Calvin, who wrote: 'By predestination we mean the Eternal Decrees of God, by which He determined with Himself whatever He wished to happen with regard to every man. All are not created on equal terms, but some are preordained to eternal life, others to eternal damnation' (*Institutes*, xxxiii. 7). John Wesley vigorously opposed this 'dreadful dogma of reprobation', and showed that the Gospels and the whole of the New Testament are against it. Many of Charles Wesley's hymns showed this same strong repudiation of the doctrine, the more so since it was his custom to print such words as '*all*' in italics when he was declaring the scope of God's salvation. For instance,

> O for a trumpet voice,
>   On *all* the world to call!
> To bid their hearts rejoice
>   In Him who died for *all*;
> For *all* my Lord was crucified.
> For *all*, for *all* my Saviour died.
>
> (*MHB* 114; cf. 75, etc.)

This dogma of predestination to salvation or damnation is now dead, except in the thought of some of the Sects; and the 'Neo-Calvinism' of Karl Barth and others has not revived it. But another dogma has taken its place; what has been called 'Calvinism-minus-God'. This atheistic determinism speaks of the absolute sovereignty, not of God, but of vast impersonal forces which are beyond human control. Its 'horrible decrees' are those of biological evolution, heredity, environment, economic law and the Totalitarian State. In attacking every form of this heresy, the preacher need not look far for appropriate texts (e.g. 2^2, Mt 11^{28}, Jn 1^{29}, 3^{16}, Rom 8^{32}, 2 Cor 5^{19}, 1 Tim 2^6).

NOTE 5. WHAT IS SIN?

(a) *All sin is against God.* To John, as to all biblical writers, 'sin' is entirely a religious concept. Not only every defiance of God, but every wrong attitude to our fellows, is an expression of 'sin' against *God* (see 5^{17}, Ps 51^4, Lk 15^{18}). Yes, all sin is against God, and the reason why so many people have no sense of sin is that they do not really believe in God. They may feel remorse or shame; they may despise themselves for living below their own standards; they may have a 'social conscience' about war, race prejudice and juvenile delinquency; but they cannot have a sense of sin if they ignore the reality of God. The unbeliever who is conscious of moral failure may resolve to make all possible reparation to those he has wronged, and to do more than his duty to them in the future—as if he could. More often, perhaps, he thrusts his sense of guilt into the subconscious and forgets all about it, thereby creating what D. M. Baillie calls 'a repressed moral-failure complex' which paralyses moral endeavour and inhibits every attempt at a new beginning (*God was in Christ*, p. 163). Somehow we preachers must convince him that all his wrongdoing is 'sin' against God, but that God is eager to forgive his past and revolutionize his future.

(b) *Sin is unbelief.* This is John's characteristic conception of sin. The coming of Christ into the world made inevitable the ultimate manifestation of sin (see Jn $5^{38, \ 40}$, 8^{24}, 16^9). It is finally demonstrated in man's rejection of the revelation of God in Christ, and in his choice of alienation from God rather than fellowship with Him (see 2^{22-3}, 3^{23}, 4^{2-3}).

(c) *Sin is egoism.* Unbelief is really egocentricity. The sinner is one who repudiates God's loving sovereignty over him and insists on being his own master; who rejects the destiny which God proposes for him, and prefers to work out his own destiny. Instead of putting God at the centre of his life, he puts himself there. It is this conception of sin as egocentric unbelief that John has in mind when he says that '*sin is lawlessness*' (3⁴; cf. Mt 7²¹, ²³. 'Iniquity' and 'law-lessness' are variant translations of the same Greek word). Sin means breaking the 'law of God', as summarized in the two supreme commandments of love and expressed in the perfect life of the human Jesus. Have done with your sophistries, says John, and accept the plain simple fact that sin means looking God in the face and shouting 'No'! '*Sin is lawlessness*'; it is high-handed rebellion against God.

(*d*) *Sin is a perversion of man's whole personality.* It is not just a part of man's being, an 'unbelieving and egocentric self' which he can isolate from the rest of him, and which his better self can defeat and destroy. It involves man's entire nature (see Mt 12³⁴, 15¹⁹). In the far-off beginnings of the human race, primitive man chose to obey his own impulses, rather than the will of God. Once that fatal choice was made, sin gained a bridgehead in human nature, and its consequences have been transmitted to every soul of man. We inherit a nature which is perverted by sin; by what we call 'original sin' in its personal aspect. We are born with a tragic bias to self-centred independence of the will and love of God. It is when we identify ourselves with these egocentric impulses that we become deliberate sinners. But this perversion of personality is not only due to 'original sin'; it is increased by every actual sin which the sinner commits. As he persists in his career of sin, he becomes less and less sensitive to its presence within him (2¹¹). Evil habits are formed which become a very part of him. What a vicious circle is here; we do what we do because we are what we are; we are what we are partly because we have done what we have done. Sin exercises a despotic tyranny over the sinner, and partly as the result of his own consent (Jn 8³⁴). Only Christ can deliver him from this dread slavery (see *Note 23*, p. 104). If sin's slavery is never broken, its final issue is spiritual death (see 5¹⁶⁻¹⁷ and *Note 26*, p. 121).

NOTE 6. SIN IN BELIEVERS

There is no New Testament support for the idea that entire sancti-fication (full salvation) immediately and miraculously follows con-version. John flatly contradicts the boast of the heretics that, in their case, this has already happened (see comments on 1⁸, ¹⁰). But this delusion is not unknown among us today. A man can have such an ecstatic experience of conversion that he imagines that he has now entirely done with sin; that he is a 'saved man' who need no longer pray—

> *Purge me from every evil blot;*
> *My idols all be cast aside;*
> *Cleanse me from every sinful thought,*
> *From all the filth of self and pride.* (*MHB* 562)

(*a*) *The believer is still a sinner, and liable to sin.* Despite some verses which seem to contradict this statement, there is plenty of evidence that, in John's judgement, the Christian is not only capable of sin, but that from time to time he does commit actual sins. See 1⁸⁻¹⁰, 2¹⁻², 5¹⁶. If sin were confined to a 'segment' of man's personality, to his 'lower self', the Christian's experience of being '*begotten of God*' (3⁹, etc.) could mean that that 'lower self' is so completely destroyed, and his 'higher self' is so divinely empowered, that future sin is out of the question. But, as we have seen in *Note 5*, sin is a radical perversion of the whole personality, and we must remember that 'personality' includes the unconscious as well as the conscious self. (On 'unconscious sin', see *Note 22*, p. 102). It follows that, while a real transformation of his whole being begins when a man is 'born from above' (see *Note 15*, p. 77), the 'old man' has an obstinate power of survival, and the struggle to master him will last the Christian his lifetime. Indeed, egoism is so all-pervasive that it insinuates itself even into our virtues. We do something which we are sure will meet with God's approval, and—we think—from the purest motive; but honest self-examination shows that we were partly moved by a desire for the praise of men, or by the hope of increasing our credit balance in the Bank of Heaven. Our very prayers can be corrupted by sin. That is why we must pray, every day, 'Forgive us our trespasses', and offer the petition,

> *Show me, as my soul can bear,*
>   *The depth of inbred sin;*
> *All the unbelief declare,*
>   *The pride that lurks within.* (*MHB* 465)

(*b*) *But the believer is expected to be sinless.* We now turn to those words of John which seem, at first sight, to contradict his assumption that the believer is still liable to sin. In 1⁷, ⁹ he says that the believer is cleansed from '*all*' sin, but he does not say when this process will be completed. But in 3⁶ he says, '*Whosoever abideth in him* [Christ] *sinneth not*'; in 3⁹ he says, '*Whosoever is begotten of God doeth no sin . . . and he cannot sin*'; and in 5¹⁸ he again says '*sinneth not*'. So the believer is still liable to sin, and yet he '*sinneth not*'; indeed he '*cannot sin*'. Perhaps the explanation of this seeming contradiction is twofold.

(i) In 2¹ the verb 'to sin' is in the aorist tense, and so refers to occasional action. The strict translation would be, 'that ye may not fall into this or that sin. And if any man does fall into this or that sin . . .'. But, in 3⁶, ⁹, 5¹⁸, John uses the verb in the present tense, and his literal meaning is that the believer does not, indeed cannot, keep on sinning. The Christian may commit a single act of sin, now and then, but he cannot be a habitual sinner. This has been called 'an almost desperate exegesis', and C. H. Dodd wonders if John's

D

readers could be expected to grasp this subtle distinction between the two tenses; but surely it is likely that, in his preaching to them, John had often made clear this distinction between an occasional act of sin, and living in sin.

(ii) In any case John is making these sweeping assertions, '*sinneth not*' and '*cannot sin*', to challenge his readers to think out the implications of their faith. 'Abiding in Christ'; 'begotten of God'. Let them think out the real meaning of these tremendous phrases. Is not this relationship with God in Christ utterly incompatible with a life of sin—or even an occasional lapse into sin? In so far as they continue, in any degree, to live in sin, they are, to that degree, not living in Christ. In so far as they behave, at any moment, as if they were still children of the Devil, it is obvious that they are not yet fully '*begotten of God*' (see 3⁸⁻¹⁰). Do they not see that the true believer can no more live in sin than the unbeliever can live out of it? Do they not see that they are *expected* to be sinless?

John's words ought to startle and challenge us. The Christian, in so far as he is a Christian, cannot sin. Is not Christ the centre of his being? Is not his Saviour ready and able to finish the work He has begun in him? Then surely every trace of sin—conscious sin, any-how—is an abnormality. The Christian is expected to have done with sin. (For 'entire sanctification' or 'perfect love', see *Note 22*, p. 102).

NOTE 7. THE WORLD

Only once in this epistle does John use '*the world*' in the sense of the physical world and its affairs (3¹⁷). Elsewhere it means 'human-ity'—the inhabitants of the created world—but in a special sense which goes back to the thought of Jesus Himself, whose ministry was based on the fact that humanity is *sinful* humanity. Men have rebelled against God (see *Note 5*, p. 35) and organized human society in defiant opposition to His will. It is this conception of '*the world*' (cf. our phrase, 'modern secularism') which John stresses throughout this epistle. '*The whole world*' lies under the domination of the Evil One (5¹⁹; cf. Jn 12³¹, 14³⁰, 16¹¹), and the Antichrist is already at work in this anti-God society (4³). But, amazing love, God '*sent his only begotten Son into the world*' (4⁹) to be '*the Saviour of the world*' (4¹⁴) and the '*propitiation*' for the sins of '*the whole world*' (2²). Christians are not to be surprised '*if the world hateth*' them (3¹³), even as it hated Christ (Jn 7⁷, 8²³, 15¹⁸, 18³⁶), but '*greater is he* [Christ] *that is in you than he* [the Evil One] *that is in the world*' (4⁴). Through faith in Christ, believers will share His victory and will '*overcome the world*' (5⁴⁻⁵. See *Note 25*, p. 114).

'*The world*' on the other side of the Iron Curtain is officially organized on the basis of a militant atheism. Apart from the Nazi revival of paganism, however, Western Civilization has not *deliber-ately* rebelled against God, or launched a large-scale attack on

Christ and His Church. Humanity, as we know it, has *drifted* away
from God and allowed Him to be crowded out of the centre of its
life. The modern Englishman 'believes' in God in a vague sort of
way—and just takes Him for granted. He says he is deeply religious
at heart, even if he isn't always talking about God. But this indifference to God is just as deadly an attitude as open defiance;
perhaps more deadly, for it tends to blind our contemporaries to
the fact that human society is still organized in fatal opposition
to the will of God. The Church must always be the Church Militant,
mobilizing all the forces of redemptive love against the evil powers
which still dominate the life of '*the world*'.

2³⁻⁶. Summary: *I have said that 'God is light', and that
means that He communicates Himself to us, so
that we can know Him. But we can only know
that we really know Him if we do His will, and if
we live a life of radiant goodness, even as Jesus did.*

The test of right living (**1⁵-2⁶**; see p. 19) comes to its climax
in **2³⁻⁶**. These verses look back to **1⁵⁻⁷**, but 'fellowship with
God' is now expressed as 'knowing God', and 'walking in the
light' as 'keeping God's commandments'.

2³. '*know we that*'. The phrase 'we know that...' occurs 15
times in *1 John*, and this note of Christian certainty comes to
tremendous climax in **5¹⁸⁻²⁰**. See *Note 27*, p. 124.

'*we know him*'. John is significantly vague in his use of 'he'
and 'him'; often we can only tell from the context whether he
refers to God or Christ. His very carelessness underlines his
contention that God is only really known in and through
Christ. Some think that the context of **2³** shows that 'him' refers
to Christ. On the contrary, in the next verse John quotes yet
another boast of the Gnostic heretics, and this boast would
certainly be 'I know *God*' (see p. 5), so that 'him' must mean
'God' in both verses. 'Knowing God' is one of the major
themes of John's Gospel and of this Epistle. What it means
is studied in *Note 8*, p. 43.

'*if we keep his commandments*'. Christian experience of God,
says John, is not a mere emotional rapture, a sentimental
doting upon God; at its heart is an exacting discipline. The
gospel is both an offer and a demand; it is the good news of
salvation, a wonderful offer of fellowship with God; it is also
a startling challenge and a tremendous demand. To '*know*'
God is to possess eternal life; it is also to be committed to a

lifetime of costly discipline. That is why so many of our contemporaries are practising atheists. The real reason why they will not come to Church is that, in its worship, they would have to encounter God and come to terms with Him. They do not *want* to 'know' God, for to have a real experience of Him would mean that they must revolutionize their lives, abandon their routine of self-centred irresponsibility, and meet the challenge to '*keep his commandments*'. As Kierkegaard said, 'It is so hard to believe, because it is so hard to obey'.

But what are the commandments of God? Jesus never elaborated them in a series of rigid rules and regulations, like those of an army barracks or a prison, to be obeyed to the letter, without thinking, and for fear of the consequences. He did not give us a New Decalogue, with a parallel series of precise 'Thou shalt's and 'Thou shalt not's, thus encouraging a New Pharisaism. John is true to the mind of Jesus when he sums up the commandments as 'believing on' Jesus Christ (3^{23}; see *Note 18*, p. 90), loving God with our whole being (2^5; see *Note 9*, p. 45), and loving our fellow-Christians (and all men) even as Jesus loves us (2^{7-11}; see *Note 11*, p. 52). And, says John, if we really '*know*' God, if we have a genuine experience of Him, our obedience to these commandments will be natural and inevitable (see *KG*, p. 100). If our obedience is half-hearted or grudging, we do not really '*know*' God; we have only a nodding acquaintance with Him. Yes; we have not really encountered Him until we have met Him on the Hill of the Cross; and, as we look at that Cross, we cannot but say, 'Thou hast done all this for me! What must I do for Thee?'— and the only possible answer is—

> *Love so amazing, so divine,*
> *Demands my soul, my life, my all.* (*MHB* 182)

We must '*keep his commandments*', therefore, without condition or reservation, and whether to do so is easy or difficult. The verb '*keep*' could almost be translated 'cherish'; His will must be our delight. A quotation from the Covenant Service of the Methodist Church is relevant. 'Christ has many services to be done; some are easy, some are difficult; some bring honour, others bring reproach; some are suitable to our natural inclinations and temporal interests, others are contrary to both. In some we may please Christ and please ourselves, in others we cannot please Christ except by denying ourselves.

Yet the power to do all these things is assuredly given to us in Christ, who strengthened us.' After this reminder, follows the pledge: 'We take upon ourselves with joy the yoke of obedience, and engage ourselves, for love of Thee, to seek and do Thy perfect will. We are no longer our own, but Thine' (*Book of Offices*, p. 131).

2⁴. '*I know him*'—so boast the heretics. But knowledge of God often meant to them intellectual propositions about God, rather than an intimate relationship with and experience of God (see *Note 8*, p. 43). Pride in such intellectual enlightenment beguiled them into imagining that they were no longer bound to obey the commandments of God and the Christian ethic; these only applied to their 'inferiors', the rank and file of the Church. Paul met such presumptuous 'knowers of God' towards the end of his ministry, and said of them, 'They profess that they know God; but by their works they deny him, being abominable and disobedient' (Tit 1¹⁶). The test of **2³** (see comment) obviously justifies John in saying that such a boaster is a '*liar*', and that '*the truth is not in him*' (see *Note 4*, p. 25).

2⁵ᵃ. '*his word*' means almost the same as '*his commandments*' (**2³⁻⁴**), as it did sometimes on the lips of Jesus (cf Jn 14¹⁵ with 14²³⁻⁴). But, if '*word*' has the wider meaning of 'gospel' as in **1¹** (see comment), '*keepeth his word*' could perhaps be paraphrased, 'liveth his life under the control of the whole message of the gospel; the total revelation of what God is, the salvation He offers, and the conduct He requires' (cf Jn 8⁵¹, 17⁶).

'*the love of God*'. As always in this letter, except in **4⁹**, this means 'our love for God'. In so far as we 'know' God and experience His amazing love for us, we must inevitably give Him the responsive love of our hearts. On 'Our love for God', see *Note 9*, p. 45.

'*perfected*'. In so far as any Christian obeys the whole will of God, he shows that he knows and loves God. But more; as his obedience becomes more and more complete, '*verily*' (i.e. really and truly, in contrast to the deluded heretics) his love for God '*is perfected*' (*AV, RSV*). John deals with this difficult idea of Perfect Love more fully in **4¹², ¹⁷⁻¹⁸**; see *Note 22*, p. 102.

2⁵ᵇ⁻⁶. '*Hereby*' refers forward to the next verse.

'*know we that*'. Here again is the note of Christian certainty; see comment on **2³**.

'*we are in him*', '*abideth in him*'; that is, in God. The Christian's relationship with God was described as 'having fellowship' with Him in **1³, ⁶**, as 'knowing' Him in **2³⁻⁴**, and as 'loving' Him in **2⁵ᵃ**. Now it is described as being '*in him*' (**2⁵ᵇ**) or, more fully, '*abiding in him*' (**2⁶**). This idea of the Christian's spiritual union with God and with Christ is another of the major concepts of John's Gospel and of this letter. It is fully studied in *Note 10*, p. 48.

'*walk even as he walked*'. The practical test changes from '*keep his commandments*' (**2³**) to '*walk as he walked*'; cf. 'walk in the light' (**1⁷**). The word translated '*he*' really means 'that one'; it is used six times in *1 John*, and always, as here, refers to *Christ*. If we are really in spiritual union with God, then in our daily behaviour we shall imitate the human life of Christ, His Son. The heretics say, 'We abide in God' (**2⁶**; again John is quoting them), but are they prepared to face this test? They cannot!

John does not mean that we are literally to imitate every detail of the unique life which Jesus lived in Palestine; for instance, that we are never to marry or take regular employment—any more than he means that we are to perform miracles, claim to be the Messiah, and literally end our days on a Cross. When Jesus had washed the feet of His disciples, He said, 'I have given you an example, that ye also should do as I have done to you' (Jn 13¹⁵), but He did not mean that they were literally to imitate His action; rather that they must imitate His life of self-giving service, of which the feetwashing was an illustration (cf. 'take up his cross' in Mk 8³⁴. See also Phil 2⁵, Eph 5²). So, when John says we are to '*walk as he walked*', he means that our behaviour must always be in harmony with the *spirit* of Christ; for instance, that we imitate His purity (3³) and His self-giving love (3¹⁶). But, since John has been writing about *obedience* (2³⁻⁵), it may be that he specially has in mind the perfect obedience of Jesus to the will of the Father, which was so prominent in his Gospel; see John 4³⁴, 5³⁰, 6³⁸, 14³¹, etc. Jesus offered this obedience on our behalf, as our Representative (see comment on 2²; cf. Rom. 5¹⁹). Now, brought into intimate union with God through what Christ has done for us, we are to make Christ's obedience the norm of our own living; to obey as He obeyed, that we may justify God in reconciling us to Himself while we were still disobedient. The adult as well as the child must pray—

> *Fain I would be as Thou art;*
> *Give me Thy obedient heart:*
> *Thou art pitiful and kind;*
> *Let me have Thy loving mind.* (*MHB* 832)

Whenever we have to make a moral decision, or decide our attitude to such social problems as war, apartheid, capital punishment, juvenile delinquency, wild-cat strikes and un-scrupulous business practices—then we are to '*walk as he walked*'; to be obedient to what we believe to be the will of God for us.

Of course, it would be ridiculous to urge anyone who is not a Christian to imitate Jesus. Even if, for twenty years, he strove to do so to the very limit of his will-power, the effort could end in nothing but despair or a nervous breakdown. It is only the man who '*abideth*' in Christ, and so '*abideth*' in God, who can be expected to imitate Christ (see Jn 15[5]).

NOTE 8. KNOWING GOD

The supreme aim of man is to know God, and thereby to find his own highest well-being. We can sympathize with the man who says: 'I'm an atheist, but I don't *like* my unbelief, or *prefer* to think that there is no God.' The man we cannot understand is the one who says, 'I'm an atheist', and then goes capering round his godless universe as though he had discovered the secret of ineffable bliss!

Knowledge of God cannot be gained by intellectual research; God can only be known as He reveals Himself to man. The Gnostic heretics accepted this truth, but claimed that God fully reveals Himself only to the select few, the true Gnostics or 'Knowers', and not to the rank and file of the Church (see p. 5 and *Note 3*, p. 23). But in John's Gospel Jesus says, again and again, that God's revelation of Himself is given to *all* who believe on His Son (Jn 8[31-2], 14[6-9], 17[3]). So, in this letter, John tests the proud claims of the 'Knowers' and finds them false (1[6], 2[4-6, 8]); he says to *all* faithful Christians, '*ye know him*' (2[13-14]), '*you all* possess knowledge' (of God. See comment on 2[20]); and, writing on behalf of all genuine believers, he says, '*We know him that is true*' (5[20]). Yes, a believer does not have to be a D.D., or go to a Theological Training College, or have private mystical visions of God, before he can '*know*' Him.

But what does 'knowing God' mean? The *gnosis* which the heretics claimed to possess was detailed spiritual knowledge *about* God, the structure of the higher world, and the way by which the Enlightened might escape into it from the lower world (see p. 5). This is not at all what the Christian means by 'knowing God'.

(1) Knowledge of God includes knowing *about* God; that He exists and what He is like. We learn something about Him as we study the world of nature and history, and listen to the voice of conscience. We learn more about Him as the message of the Bible is explained to us in home, school and church. When we become serious students of the Bible, we realize that, though Moses and the prophets have told us much about God, no one has spoken about Him with such authority as Jesus Himself. Indeed, as we study the Gospels, we realize that God has written His own autobiography; that, in the person of His Son, He has lived out His character in a human life, so that all men may know what He is like; that Jesus was speaking utter truth when He said: 'He that hath seen me hath seen the Father' (Jn 14[9]). Now we know all that mortals will ever need to know *about* God; that He is just like Jesus Christ.

(2) But 'knowing' a person means far more than knowing all *about* him. You may know a lot about Albert Schweitzer, or Malcolm Sargent, or Tony Hancock; you may have read biographies or articles about them; you may even have 'seen' them on television; but, if you have never met them, you cannot say that you really 'know' them. Real knowledge is based on close personal relationship. It is more than intellectual knowledge; it is the heart-to-heart knowledge of intimate friendship; it is what has been called the I-Thou knowledge of personal experience. When a man and his wife love each other so deeply that there is no reserve in their self-giving; when their intimacy is so real that they can unburden their hearts to each other about their holiest thoughts and their fiercest temptations, about their noblest longings and their shabbiest desires—then, in a real sense, they 'know' each other.

Just so, in the Old Testament, knowing God does not mean knowing about God by speculating about His attributes (Job 11[7]); it means having personal experience of God through entering into intimate relations with Him. In so far as a man recognized the saving activity of God in his life, gave Him complete trust and devotion and willingly obeyed His every command, he could 'know' God (Jer 22[16], Hos 6[3]). The Hebrews did not 'know' God, said the prophets, because, in disobeying Him, they refused to have true relations with Him (Isa 1[3], Jer 9[6], Hos 4[1]; cf. Jn 8[54-5]). That is why, in the Old Testament, knowledge of God is always something yet to be possessed, in the future (Isa 11[9], 52[6], Jer 31[34]).

But the message of the New Testament is that those who 'know' Jesus Christ can, in a very real sense, 'know' God, and *here and now*. When Jesus said that no man could 'know the Father, save the Son, and to whomsoever the Son willeth to reveal him' (Mt 11[27]), and that 'he that hath seen me hath seen the Father' (Jn 14[9]), He meant far more than that He could tell people everything *about* God (see para (1), above). He meant that, since He was the Son of God, God incarnate, the man who 'knows' Him, really and truly 'knows' God (Jn 14[7]). To 'know' Christ is to have personal experience of Him and of His amazing and inexhaustible love, to respond to that love in complete trust and self-committal, and, in intimate union with Him, to live a life of devotion and obedience. But to know Christ like that is to know God (Jn 17[3]), and the test of this knowledge is our response of devotion and the disciplined life of obedience (see 1[6], 2[4]).

It follows that this knowledge of God is not the privileged experience of a mere handful of people in a generation; nor do we have to master the complete works of Thomas Aquinas, John Calvin, John Wesley and Karl Barth before we can say: 'Now, at long last, I know God.' Millions of Christians, most of them plain, ordinary folk like you and me, have rejoiced in this common experience of God. High Churchmen, Low Churchmen, Methodists and Presbyterians, Roman Catholics and Quakers—Mrs Jenny Morton spoke for them all in her BBC debate with Mrs Margaret Knight, when she said: 'I am absolutely certain of my faith and live in relationship with God, as other Christians do. This is not a theory; it is an experience.' Pascal put it quite simply when he said: 'To know God, you must love Him' (cf. 4[8]).

Our knowledge of God will never be complete in this life; but, as we increase in devotion and obedience, we shall know God more and more fully, until that day when we know Him even as, all along, we have been known by Him (1 Cor 13[12]).

NOTE 9. OUR LOVE FOR GOD

Every loyal Jew knew that human devotion to God is the very essence of real religion. Perhaps that is why, as far as our records go, Jesus spoke of man's love for God only in Mark 12[30] = Matthew 22[37], Matthew 24[12], Luke 11[42], John 5[42], and why Paul mentioned it only in Romans 8[28], 1 Corinthians 2[9], 8[3]. In contrast, in the five chapters of *1 John* our love for God is mentioned 14 times. This stress was necessary because love for God, and its expression in love for their fellows, was markedly absent from the teaching and life of the heretics. John does not mention the Christian's love for Christ, but he assumes that we can only truly love God as we know and love His Son; that has been made quite clear in his Gospel (see Jn 8[42], 14[15, 21, 23-4, 28], 16[27], 21[15-17]).

Our love for God is plainly mentioned in 4[20-1], 5[1-2], but the phrase '*the love of God*' is ambiguous. In 4[9] it clearly means God's love for us; elsewhere it probably means our love for God (see 2[5, 15], 3[17], 5[3]). So, in 4[12, 17, 18], '*his love*' and '*love*' also mean our love for God.

One common Greek work for 'love' was '*eros*', made familiar to us by the statue in Piccadilly Circus. The word had many meanings—sexual desire was only one of them—but in every aspect it stood for a longing to possess an object because it is attractive and therefore desirable. Self was always at the centre of '*eros*'; its every activity was some form of self-interest and self-aggrandizement. The New Testament writers realized that '*eros*' was a quite unsuitable word to express what Jesus meant by 'love'. They therefore rejected it, and used instead the word '*agapē*'. This old word was rarely used by the Greeks, and meant 'to like', 'to esteem', 'to prefer'. The New Testament writers took this 'cool and colourless word' and filled it with a new meaning; with what Jesus meant when He spoke of love, and what He revealed about love when, for love of man, He died for him on the Cross. So John says, '*Hereby know we love, because he laid down his life for us*' (3[16]); and again, '*Herein is love, not that we loved God, but that he loved us*' (4[10]). Yes; if we want to know what '*agapē*' is, we shall not think of *our* love for our home folk and our closest friends, and of the highest love of which we are capable, our love for God—and then say, 'That love, broadened and deepened, must be something like God's love for us.' As Dostoevsky made one of his characters say: 'Jesus died because of love, but what do you and I know about it? We who prattle of love, blind as to what it is, reducing it to some small humdrum notion of being kind.' It is when we think of the amazing love of God for us which was expressed in the Incarnation and which came to climax on the Hill of Calvary, that we stand, dumb-struck with wonder, at the foot of that Cross and whisper to ourselves: 'That is love! How paltry is my noblest conception of it, compared with that!' And so we see that '*agapē*' in contrast to '*eros*', 'seeketh not its own'; its whole concern is for the welfare of others; it is pure self-giving, and to the uttermost.

We use the word 'love' for a host of attitudes and feelings, ranging from the sub-animal to the sublime. As Lord Elton once said: 'If Romeo and the latest winner of the Dunmow Flitch and Oscar Wilde and St Francis of Assisi can all be said to "love", no one who uses the word can be certain what meaning he will convey.' It is a capital misfortune that we have no English word to translate what the Christian means by '*agapē*'. The word 'charity' (*AV*) is now spoiled, for its meaning has been degraded. The best we can do is to speak of 'Christian love'.

But there are three kinds of '*agapē*'; God's love for us (see *Note 16*, p. 79), our love for God, and our love for our fellows. The three have in common this quality of utter self-giving; but they differ from each other, as we see when we examine them. Here we are thinking of the Christian's love for God, and Nygren is right when he says that God's love for us differs from our love for God, in that God's love for man is spontaneous and uncaused by any quality in the character of man (see *Note 16*), whereas our love for God is always 'caused'. But in what sense? Is it caused by the fact that God is man's Creator? No, man's nature is so perverted by sin that it is not natural to him to 'love' the God who has made and sustained him. Indeed, man's 'natural' attitude to God is one of hatred (see Mk 12[7], Lk 19[14], Jn 3[20], 7[7], 15[18], Rom 5[10], Col 1[21]); a hatred which came to its most terrible manifestation in the Cross. Is it caused by man's fear of the consequences of this hatred? A man may say to himself, 'I *ought* to love God. It will be the worse for me if I don't. I will do my best to love Him'; but that is a higher form of '*eros*' and not '*agapē*' at all. The man is forcing himself to 'love' God that he may avoid divine retribution, and ensure a happy heaven hereafter as reward for having done his duty to God. But there is no self-seeking in '*agapē*'.

John shows us in what sense our love for God is a 'caused' love, when he says, '*We love, because he first loved us* (4[19]). The Authorized Version translates 'We love *him*', that is, *God*, but that is not the reading of the best MSS. In view of 4[20a], however, it is probable that John specially has in mind our love for God. He says that our very capacity to love has been 'caused', called out, by the amazing love which God has shown to us. This truth, that man's love for God is his grateful response to God's love for him, is foreshadowed in the Old Testament. The whole argument of Deuteronomy 6[4-25] is that the Hebrews must love and serve God *because* of the love which He has shown to them, especially in redeeming them from the slavery of Egypt at the Exodus. But the Christian's love for God is 'caused' by a far greater redemption, by an even more remarkable revelation of God's love. It is when, with increasing wonder, we follow Christ to the end of His costly, self-giving ministry, and at last stand awe-struck at the foot of the Cross, and then hear the Risen Christ engage Himself to us for ever as He says, Lo, I am with you alway'—it is then that we cry,

> *Amazing love! how can it be*
> *That Thou, my God, shouldst die for me?* (*MHB* 371).

And it is then that wondering gratitude quickens us to responsive love for God, and we offer Him the passionate self-giving of a wholly committed and dedicated personality—feeling, mind and will; they are all included in our love for Him. It is then that we cry,

> *Love so amazing, so divine,*
> *Demands my soul, my life, my all.* (*MHB* 182; cf. 437,546.)

At first, a self-regarding element may survive in our love for God —some unworthy calculation about what God will do for those who serve Him—but the more we 'survey the wondrous Cross', the more pure and selfless our love becomes, until at last we can cry,

> *My God, I love thee—not because*
> *I hope for heaven thereby,*
> .   .   .
> *But as Thyself hast loved me,*   .   .
> *O ever-loving Lord.* (*MHB* 446.)

On the 'perfecting' of our love for God, see *Note 22*, p. 102. On its issue in love for our fellows, see *Note 11*, p. 52.

NOTE 10. UNION WITH GOD IN CHRIST

Through 'believing on' Jesus Christ (see *Note 18*, p. 90), the Christian enters into a new relationship with God which is variously described in *1 John* as 'fellowship with God', 'knowing God', and 'being born of God'. But, more often, John describes this relationship as one of intimate personal *union* with Christ and God, a union which is expressed by the phrase '*abiding in*' or '*being* in' Christ or God. Paul had expressed this intimate oneness of the Christian with Christ in such phrases as dying with Christ, rising with Him, and living with Him in newness of life (Rom 6[3-11], etc.), and often his famous phrase 'in Christ' was a sort of shorthand summary of this dying-rising-and-living with Christ (Rom 6[11], 8[1], 1 Cor 1[30], 2 Cor 5[17]). John would be familiar with Paul's thought, but his conception of the Christian's union with Christ is not a development of Paul's 'in Christ'—in some respects it differs from it; it is closely related to the teaching of Jesus in John's Gospel.

Jesus often spoke of the true believer as '*abiding in*' or '*being in*' Him (Jn 6[56], 14[20], 15[4, 5, 7]), and this truth is stressed in 2[5, 6, 24, 27, 28], 3[6], 5[20]. John is also true to the mind of Jesus when he makes no difference between 'abiding in *Christ*' and 'abiding in *God*' (cf. 2[24], 5[20] with Jn 17[21]; see also 4[13, 15, 16]). But our union with God in Christ is a reciprocal, not a one-way, relationship. So Jesus said that the believer 'abideth in me, and I in him' (Jn 6[56]), and often spoke of 'Ye in me, and I in you' (Jn 14[20]; cf. Jn 15[4-5]). John also stresses this reciprocal relationship in 3[24], 4[12-13, 15-16].

What a wonderful intimacy is this! The Christian lives in, abides in, Christ; Christ lives in, abides in, the Christian. But what is the nature of this faith-union? It is not a union which is only experienced in occasional, ecstatic raptures (e.g. 2 Cor 12[1-4]). The very word '*abideth*' which Jesus used of our union with Him, and which John also stresses, reminds us of the continuity and permanency of our communion with God. It is not a rare and transient rapture, but a constant experience, daily renewed through a lifetime. It is true that, in the bustle of daily life, we are not always *conscious* of this oneness with God in Christ, and that, in the sacrament of the Lord's Supper, we have a very special experience of 'Holy Communion' with Him; but always, whenever the Christian stops to think about Christ, he can say, 'He abides in me, and I in Him'.

Nor is this faith-union with Christ the privilege of a select minority of mystics who are peculiarly sensitive to the divine presence. Just as *all* Christians, says John, can 'know' God, so he says of *every* believer, '*God abideth in him, and he in God*' (4¹⁵).

The aim of the 'pure' mystic is to achieve a union with God in which his human spirit is *absorbed* into the divine Being. This is *not* what John means by 'You in Him, and He in you'. In unreserved trust and love, the believer identifies himself with God who, in the life, death and risen ministry of Christ, has so wonderfully identified Himself with us; but, in doing so, the Christian does not *lose* his identity. So, immediately after saying 'No longer I, but Christ liveth in me', Paul goes on to say, 'and that life which I now live, I live in faith' (Gal 2²⁰). The I-Thou relationship still continues. The Christian is not absorbed into the being of God; rather his personality is enriched with new powers by the indwelling Christ— powers which enable him to do the divine will more perfectly. So John says that the Christian who '*abideth in*' Christ has an increased, rather than a diminished responsibility as an individual; he must walk as Jesus walked (2⁶), live without sin (3⁶), keep God's commandments (3²⁴) and love his fellows (4¹², ¹⁶).

This union is not a static union, realized once and for all at the hour of conversion. It is a relationship which becomes more and more intimate and life-transforming as we become more and more 'at one' with Christ, and it will not be consummated until we enter the Hereafter (3²⁻³; cf. Phil 1²³). This deepening communion has been the joy and inspiration of Christians through the centuries. The secret of the radiant lives of the saints has been that they knew that, in them, Christ had fulfilled His promise, 'I in you, and you in Me'; and we can share that transforming experience. We, too, can sing with Bernard of Clairvaux,

> *Jesu, our only joy be Thou,*
> *As Thou our prize wilt be;*
> *Jesu, be Thou our glory now,*
> *And through eternity.* (*MHB* 108)

We, too, can sing with Charles Wesley,

> *So shall we ever live, and move,*
> *And be with Christ in God.* (*MHB*, 383; cf. 110, etc.)

And only in so far as that prayer is answered, shall we Christians be able to match the need of our day and make a saving impact upon our secular society.

(b) 2⁷⁻¹⁷. The Test of Genuine Loving

Starting from the fact that 'The Christian life is a life of fellowship with God', John has given the first test by which his readers may judge whether or not they are living that life; the test of Right Living (**1⁵–2⁶**). He now applies the second test, that of Genuine Loving—and in particular argues that 'loving the brethren' is a basic feature of the Christian life, and that love for God is incompatible with love for 'the world'.

> **2⁷⁻¹¹. Summary:** *To 'walk in the light' is to obey Christ's commandment of love to God and man; a commandment which is both old and new. But the man who says, 'I am enlightened', and rejects this imperative, is still groping in the darkness.*

2⁷. The commandments of God (see **2³⁻⁴**) were summed up by Jesus in two comprehensive imperatives: 'Love God with all your being', and 'Love your neighbour as yourself' (Mk 12³⁰⁻¹). John has mentioned the first in **2⁵** (see *Note 9*, p. 45); he now turns to the second. The commandment to love your fellow man, says John, is *'no new commandment'*; it is no novel and minor addition to the original gospel, as the loveless behaviour of the heretics would seem to presuppose (see comment on **2⁹**). It is an *'old commandment'*. It goes back to the Law of Moses (Lev 19¹⁸) and it was endorsed by Jesus Himself, so that, *'from the beginning'* of your life as Christians, you have *'heard'* it preached to you. It is the basis of the ethical life of the Christian (see *Note 11*, p. 52).

2⁸. *'Again'* (*EVV*) should be 'Yet'. It is an *'old commandment'* and 'yet' it is a *'new'* one, and this statement is doubly true. (1) *'It is true in him'*, that is, in the light of Christ's life and teaching. Did not Jesus say, again and again, 'It was said . . . but I say . . .'? Did He not come to inaugurate the new Age of Light and to make all things new? John is thinking of the words of John 13³⁴: 'A *new* commandment I give unto you, that ye love one another; even as I have loved you.' Jesus took the old command and made it *'new'* by giving it a deeper meaning and a new standard of reference—His own life of utter self-giving. 'As I have loved you'; that is what made it *'new'*. (2) It is also true *'in you'*, that is, in the experience of the readers. The age of *'darkness is passing away'* (see Jn 1⁹) and they are living in the new age of the God of Light (see *Note 3*, p. 23); and in that light, the light of Christ's guiding presence, they are ever discovering new ways in which Christ's new commandment must be applied in their present relationships with their fellows. As their conscience is enlightened, they find *new* meaning, *new* challenge, *new* demands in that 'even as I loved you'. The Christian's conscience is always in need of this fuller enlightenment. In the fifteenth century, Columbus, on one of his voyages, could write to his king, 'In the name of the Holy Trinity, from here we can send as many slaves as can be sold'! Writing about religious persecution, Lecky said, 'Philip II of Spain and Isabella inflicted more suffering in obedience to their consciences than did Nero and Domitian in obedience to their lusts'! So, in our own day, Christ's commandment is still '*new*' to us; we must re-interpret it, and apply it to all the new situations and problems of modern life.

2⁹. Now we see why Jesus stresses the test of genuine loving, here and throughout this letter. The heretics were individualists, with very little sense of social obligation; theirs was a thin-lipped, loveless intellectualism, and they arrogantly despised their less sophisticated brethren. As privileged 'Knowers' of God and of things celestial, they claimed to be exempt from obedience to God's commandments (2⁴⁻⁶); this obligation was binding only on ordinary, uninitiated Christians. In particular, they ignored the primary Christian duty of love for the brethren. Indeed, using only black and white, John speaks of the heretic who boasts 'I am enlightened' and yet '*hateth his brother*'. He rejects the God of Light, and so lives in the '*darkness*' of disobedience and sin.

2¹⁰. In the heat of theological controversy with heretics, it is dangerously possible for the orthodox to forget that Christ requires them to love their opponents, even while they hate their false teaching. So, in Revelation 2²⁻⁴, the Seer says that Christ congratulates the Church in Ephesus for her intolerance of heresy, but has this against her, 'that thou didst leave thy first love'. In no circumstances are we exempt from the duty of loving as Christ loved. Only he who '*loveth his brother*' abideth in Christ (see *Note 10*, p. 48) and so '*abideth in the light*'. The test of living in fellowship with God is that of genuine loving (see *Note 11*, p. 52).

2¹¹. As John has said (2⁹), the man who fails to love his brother '*is*' in the darkness; and the fact that something is fundamentally wrong with him is seen in his everyday behaviour, for he '*walketh*' in the darkness. He gropes and stumbles his way through life, not knowing whither he is going (cf Jn 12[35], Lk 6[39]), for pride and prejudice have blinded him to the simple fact that the only true goal of the Christian is perfect love to God *and man*.

NOTE 11. LOVE FOR OUR BRETHREN

Jesus indissolubly joined together love for God and love for our fellow man, and John stresses this essential unity throughout *1 John*. If we imagine, as did the heretics of his day, that our attitude to God has nothing to do with our attitude to our fellow man, that Christianity is a mystical religion which has no necessary moral and social application, we deceive ourselves. A 'social gospel' which is nothing but 'social' is futile; but equally futile is a personal piety which ignores our relationship to our fellows and has no concern for their spiritual and physical welfare. If we love God, we must love our fellows—and why?

Because God *commands* us to do so. So John writes, '*This commandment have we from him* [God], *that he who loveth God love his brother also*' (4[21]; see also 3[11, 23], 2 Jn 5). But how can God command us to love people? Isn't that like ordering a man and a woman to fall in love with each other? Yes; if 'love' were a mere emotion; but, as we have seen (*Note 9*, p. 45), '*agapē*' is an attitude of the whole personality, which issues in a deliberate activity of the will. 'Loving' our fellows can perhaps be best defined as 'having a deep concern for' or 'caring for' them. It is much more than vague good-will or genial affability. It means a sustained effort to discover the essential needs of others, and to further their highest well-being as fervently as we look after our own interests; indeed, as we shall see, it goes even farther than 'as thyself'. Such '*agapē*' can be and is required of us by God; and if we obey His command, we prove that we really love Him (4[7, 20]; cf. Jn 13[35]).

In the Synoptic Gospels, Jesus often illustrated the principle of 'Love thy neighbour' to show how it should be applied in concrete situations (see Mt 5-6, 18, 25[31-46]). Paul also quoted the one command of love (Gal 5[14]), but showed its implications in detail in Romans 12-15, 1 Corinthians 13, Colossians 3[18]-4[1], and Ephesians 5[22]-6[9]. By contrast, in neither Gospel nor Epistles does John deal with the outworking of the principle of '*agapē*' in any detail. It has been suggested (*WFH*, p. 179) that the reason may be that, by the end of the first century, there was a growing tendency to turn Christianity into a legal code similar to that of the Jewish Pentateuch. It was perhaps to discourage this codification of the Christian ethic into a system of regulations that John re-emphasized the single, comprehensive command of love for man, and added very little to it. Tradition says that when, in extreme feebleness, the aged John had to be carried into church, his message to the congregation was always the same: 'Little children, love one another.' When asked why he never said anything more, he replied: 'Because it is the commandment of the Lord; and because, when this is done, all is done.' Compare Augustine's famous saying: 'Love and do what you will.'

This divine command should not be *'grievous'* (5³). Giving ourselves to God in utter devotion (see *Note 9*, p. 45), we are *'begotten of God'* (4⁷) and begin to live a new sort of life (3¹⁴) whose dominant characteristic is *'agapē'*, for it is God's life and *'God is love'* (4⁸). The man who does not love his brother is *'not of God'* (3¹⁰). So the real Christian not only *must* love his brother man; he cannot help doing so.

But when John says *'Beloved, if God so loved us, we also ought to love one another'* (4¹¹), that *'so'* reminds us that Christ has given 'love' a new and deeper content (see comment on 2⁷⁻⁸). We are to love one another, even as Christ loves us; and that certainly means that we are to love *all* people, without exception, for Christ's love was never limited to any closed circle. He gave Himself to everybody, without discrimination, even as God does, and He has bidden us do the same (e.g. Mt 5⁴³⁻⁸). But is it not true that, whenever John tells us to love *'one another'* or our *'brethren'*, he is referring to our fellow Christians, and not to mankind in general? That is true, and we shall see why; but John never suggests that we should love *only* them. Has he not told us to *'walk even as he* [Christ] *walked* (2⁶), and could a man who wrote John 3¹⁶, and who added *'the whole world'* to 2², advocate a narrow, sectarian brotherliness? Did the man who wrote 3¹⁶ narrow *'us'* and *'brethren'* to mean Church members only? No; when Saul Kane, in Masefield's *Everlasting Mercy*, says of his conversion experience,

> *I knew that Christ had given me birth*
> *To brother all the souls on earth,*

he says what John would expect every Christian to be able to say, *'We love, because he first loved us'* (4¹⁹); there are no numerical limits to such a love.

It was in the fellowship of the Church, however, that the early Christians disciplined themselves to practise the supreme virtue of *'agapē'* among themselves. Here they began to break down every 'wall of partition' that separated them from one another—every barrier of breeding, rank, wealth, education, race and colour—and learnt to love one another with Christian love. And then they went out into 'the world' to live this new life of costly love and extravagant self-giving among their pagan contemporaries, who thereby recognized them as Christ's men (Jn 13³⁵, Acts 4¹³) and cried in

E

wonder: 'See how these Christians love.' But John was now faced with the alarming fact that this could no longer be said about some of the Christians of his diocese. The heretics were notorious for their unbrotherliness, but they had left the society. What was even more serious was the fact that, in the heat of controversy, some of the faithful had failed in their duty of love to their opponents (cf. Rev 2[2, 4]), and perhaps were lacking in generosity and good-will towards those who had shown some sympathy with the heretics but had remained within the society. It was to expose this dangerous, sub-Christian behaviour, and with the Church's mission to the world in mind, that again and again in this letter John urges his readers to '*love one another*'.

We cannot ignore the fact that 'See how these Christians love' has become a word of ridicule on the lips of the critics of the Church, and with some justification. How often tempers, jealousies, resentments and prejudices spoil our relationships with one another. How often cliques and 'the awkward squad' ruin committee meetings and make a mockery of John 17[21]. Even our convictions are sometimes used by the Devil to drive us apart from our fellow Christians. What havoc can be worked in Church life by the censorious puritan, the pugnacious pacifist, the extreme sacerdotalist or the bigoted fundamentalist and modernist. And what of the 'unhappy divisions' which still persist between the different denominations? John has much to say to us. Not until we take his message to heart shall we be able, with conviction and authority, to preach to mankind a gospel of universal love, and by our example present a strong challenge to a world which is tragically divided by class warfare, narrow nationalism, iron curtains and colour bars.

2[12-14]. Summary: *Some of you have recently come to doubt whether you are Christians in the fullest meaning of the word. But it is because you are already experiencing the privileges of the Christian life, and that I may encourage you to experience them more fully—the forgiveness of sins, knowledge of God, and victory over the powers of evil—that I am writing this letter.*

These verses are a parenthesis, and they present some difficulties, but their general meaning is plain. John pauses to address himself more personally to the members of his 'diocese'. The teaching of the heretics has disturbed the confidence of some of them, and made them wonder if they are really 'Christians', or—as the 'highbrows' have probably told them—mere babes in Christ. John tells them that his whole message to them is grounded on the *fact*—a fact about which he has no doubt—that they are already experiencing the privileges which the gospel offers to men. These privileges are summed up as forgiveness of sins, knowledge of God, and victory over the powers of evil. Then, without doubt, they are genuine Christians. Now let them go forward to experience even more fully the glorious possibilities of the Christian life about which John is writing. Some of our people today are strangers to this basic Christian experience, although they call themselves 'Christians'. Others have known something of it, but need to be recalled to the enthusiasm and confidence which it once gave to them.

John gives two sequences, beginning '*I write unto you*'—or, better, '*I am writing unto you*' (2^{12-13b}), and '*I have written unto you*' (2^{13c-14}). What does John mean by '*I have written*'? Some think that he is referring to a previous letter which has been lost; others that he may be referring to his Gospel. Neither suggestion is satisfactory. More probably, he is thinking of what he has already written in this letter. But why does he repeat himself in this way, for 2^{13c-14} contains very little which is not in 2^{12-13b}? Perhaps it is a rather cumbersome way of saying: 'In writing to you, I am basing my appeal on certain facts of your Christian experience—indeed, this is obvious from what I have already written.'

Each of these two sequences contains three statements, addressed to '*children*', '*fathers*' and '*young men*'. Is John addressing himself to three age-groups in the Church? If so, the order '*children*', '*fathers*', '*young men*' is strange. Again, it is said of both 'children' and 'fathers' that they '*know*' the eternal God. Also, forgiveness of sins (2^{12}) is not specially appropriate to young children. But throughout the letter the aged John thinks of *all* the Christians of Asia Minor as his sons in the faith, and calls them '*little children*' in $2^{1, 28}$, $3^{7, 18}$, 4^4, 5^{21}—and surely also in 2^{12-13}. So, if '*little children*' refers to *all* his readers, we are left with two specified groups, '*fathers*' and '*young men*'; and probably the distinction is not between seniors and juniors in age, but between those who are young in Christian experience and those who are more mature. But John does not suggest that it is *only* to new converts that Christ gives victory over evil, or that it is *only* mature Christians who come to know God; as he says elsewhere in his letter, these are the privileges of all Christians. His thought in

2¹²⁻¹⁴ may be summarized: All of you began your life in Christ with the forgiveness of your sins, and this forgiveness is available so long as the sin that remains is confessed. All of you, through your union with Christ, have come to know the eternal Father, though this is a growing knowledge which comes to its fullness in you *'fathers'*, you more mature Christians. To all of you, the Christian life is a constant conflict against the powers of evil—a conflict which may be fiercest when you are *'young'* in the faith—but through Christ you are winning the victory (see *GGF*, pp. 188-91).

2¹². *'your sins are forgiven'*. See comment on **1⁹**.

'for his name's sake'. In Jewish and Christian thought, the 'name' of God was used as equivalent to His character or person as He manifests Himself to men. Here *'his'* refers to Christ, and *'for his name's sake'* means 'because of what Christ is, and because of what He has done for you'.

2¹³. *'him which is from the beginning'* may refer to Christ (cf. Jn 1¹), but more probably refers to God the Father. As to what John means by 'knowing' God, see *Note 7*, p. 38. On *'the evil one'*, see *Note 13*, p. 67. On *'overcome'* and the victory of the Christian, see *Note 25*, p. 114.

2¹⁴. *'the word of God'*. See comment on **1¹⁰**.

NOTE 12. THE EVIL ONE

'Satan' is a Hebrew word which means 'accuser' or 'adversary', and the Greek *'diabolos'* (=Devil) has the same meaning. Satan as a superhuman person appears in only three late Old Testament passages (Job 1-2, Zech 3¹⁻², 1 Chr 21¹), but already we can see the beginning of that 'Rake's Progress' (as G. B. Caird calls it) in which Satan, the servant of God who acts as Public Prosecutor in the heavenly court, finally becomes the Devil, the arch-enemy of God and man. By the time of Jesus, the Jews believed that Satan was originally one of the higher angels, but that he began to assert his will against that of God and finally led an angelic rebellion against God. As a result of this sin of pride, he and his fellow-conspirators were banished from heaven. Satan became the superhuman adversary of mankind. By tempting primeval man and woman, in the guise of the serpent, to sin against God, he originated evil in human life, and ever since then his deadly purpose has been to ruin the human race. Jesus seems to have accepted this conception of the Devil and of his dark angels, the demons. He called the Devil 'the prince of this world' (Jn 12³¹; see also *Note 7*, p. 38), through whose tyranny men are held in bondage to sin (Jn 8³⁴), thereby becoming the children of the Devil rather than of God (Jn 8⁴⁴). From the beginning of Christ's ministry, Satan, the prince of the kingdom of evil, resisted with all his power the purpose of Jesus to establish the Kingdom of God on earth (Mt 4¹⁻¹¹, Mk 4²⁴, etc.), and Christ counter-attacked with the power of unconquerable love, until He won the final victory on the Cross (see *Note 17*, p. 82).

John's thought about the Devil (or '*evil one*') is in close harmony with that of Jesus. He says that '*the devil sinneth from the beginning*' (3⁸); before the first man was created, the Devil rebelled against God and became the arch-sinner. He is the original cause of all the sin of men, and they who surrender to his dominion are '*of the devil*' (3⁸); they become '*the children of the devil*' (3¹⁰), just as Cain did (3¹²). So completely has the Devil tyrannized mankind that '*the whole world lieth in the evil one*' (5¹⁹); that is, is under the dominion of the 'prince of this world' (cf. Lk 4⁵⁻⁸). The Son of God came into the world '*that he might destroy the works of the devil*' (3⁸). The man who accepts Him as Saviour, and is 'begotten of God', is delivered from Satan's power, for '*the evil one toucheth him not*' (5¹⁸), and he can claim to have '*overcome the evil one*' (2¹³⁻¹⁴; see *Note 25*, p. 114).

But is the Devil a real person, or is he only a 'myth', a pictorial representation of the dread reality of those evil powers which tyrannize the human race? Many modern theologians have denied the personality of the Devil, because they thought it introduced an ultimate dualism into the universe—but this is not so. In the Christian view, the Devil has not, like God, an eternal existence. He is a created being, a fallen angel; not another god, absolute in his own power. His dominion over man is only a temporary tyranny, and God has already pronounced sentence of doom against him. Chesterton may have exaggerated when he said that there is more evidence for the existence of a personal Devil than for that of a personal God, but surely belief in the diabolical personality rests on the same general facts of experience as belief in the divine personality. The difference is, as Percy Gardner said, that the latter belief is comforting, while the former is disturbing.

That raises a question. Is modern disbelief in Satan a case of wishful thinking, since a Devil who is a real person is much more terrifying than any evil 'tendency' or 'impulse'? Is this the Devil's masterpiece of deceit, that he has convinced modern man that he does not exist; that he is just an outgrown superstition, to be ignored by enlightened people? Certainly, in the earlier part of this century, the demonic powers of the 'spiritual underworld' were neglected by both theologians and preachers. Today, however, two world wars, the rise of Nazism and Russian Communism, the moral deterioration of our age and the threat of an unconsecrated omnicompetent science have shown that evil on a world scale is a terrible reality in modern life. Indeed, an increasing number of us have a feeling that this diabolical evil is not haphazard and chaotic; that there is a drive and direction and purposefulness about it which suggest a living intelligence behind it, co-ordinating these dread outbursts from the spiritual underworld. In *Nature, Man and God*, William Temple said: 'Personally I believe he [Satan] exists and that a large share of responsibility (for human evil) belongs to him and to subordinate evil spirits.' Whether we agree with him, or prefer to think of the Devil as the personification of those forces of evil which are the cumulative effect of centuries of godless self-centred living, we must not underestimate the satanic power of evil in human life.

> **2¹⁵⁻¹⁷. Summary:** *Some of you may still be attracted by what pagan society offers you, but love of God and love of 'the world' are mutually exclusive. Centre your life, not in this transient world, but in the eternal order.*

2¹⁵. '*Love not the world*' is not a plea for otherworldliness, as if '*the world*' meant the material universe, and as if John held a Gnostic view of the evil of matter (see p. 5). In later ages, narrow puritans took this text to mean that life on earth was to be regarded as a 'weary pilgrimage' through a 'vale of woe', a 'barren desert'; that physical appetites and secular interests, if they were enjoyed at all, were at best harmless relaxations from the one serious business of life, which was to make, and to help others to make, an elaborate preparation for the future glory of the next world. This is *not* what John means. God made the natural world as man's home and pronounced it 'good', and when His Son lived a human life He found high delight in it. He rejoiced in its beauty, and everywhere saw tokens of God's loving providence. He did not despise physical appetites and refuse all invitations to supper parties. He did not live the life of a hermit; He loved the companionship of men, women and children, and their everyday life— their home life, their social activities, their trade and agriculture —was of absorbing interest to Him. And it was from Jesus that John had learnt that, on this earth and in the midst of human society, we can anticipate the glory of 'eternal life'.

As we have seen in *Note 7*, p. 38, John uses '*the world*' in a special sense, as human society organized in rebellious opposition to the will of God, and under the domination of the 'prince of this world'. Here the phrase stands for what we

should call godless secularism or worldliness; for a society
whose recognized customs and conventions, standards and
ambitions, are contrary to the divine purpose. Such a society
is hostile, not only to Christ but also to the Christian, and
John was writing in an age when fierce persecution was an
imminent probability. Already the Christians were an unpopular minority (3^{13}), and in a few years Emperor Domitian
would attempt to exterminate the Church. The heretics, with
their 'modern theology', were accommodating their doctrines
to those of pagan thought, but it looks as if their policy of
compromise was being extended to their ethical behaviour, for
John says that they are '*of the world*' (4^5; cf. 2 Tim 4^{10}). But,
says John, there can be no compromise; loving 'the world'
and loving God are mutually exclusive. '*If any man love the
world, the love of (for) the Father is not in him.*' We are reminded of the words of Jesus: 'Ye cannot serve God and
mammon' (Mt 6^{24}).

Today we are living in a society which still gives primary
place, not to God but to material values and worldly ambitions, and whose standards and policies are often in deadly
opposition to the rule of God; but we must not evacuate from
'*the world*' in order to escape its fascinations or its hostility.
We must live in it and always meet the temptation to conform
to its standards with that faith which will enable us to '*overcome the world*' (5^4; cf. Rom 12^2).

2^{16}. John now defines '*the things that are in the world*' (2^{15});
and here we must remember that his warning applies, not only
to the obvious 'worldling' but also the Christian in so far as
he fails to resist the invasion of the worldly spirit into his own
heart and into the life of the Church.

'*the lust of the flesh*' means more than sexual passion. The
'*flesh*' is unregenerate human nature, and '*the lust of the flesh*'
means all the self-centred and unsanctified longings of the man
whose nature is perverted by evil, and who has not been born
from above and become a new man in Christ. In its more
'respectable' forms, it includes all the ambitions of the materi-
alist, as well as bad temper, irritability, laziness and jealousy;
in its grosser forms, covetousness, greed and every form of
sensual excess. What Virginia Woolf once said of the characters
in certain novels can be said of many of our contemporaries:
'The destiny to which they travel so luxuriously becomes more

and more unquestionably an eternity of bliss in the very best hotel in Brighton.'

'*the lust of the eyes*' means the longing for the superficial delights of life. The worldling is captivated by the glittering and glamorous, and judges everything by its outward show, regardless of its real value. He is fascinated by the gaudy prizes which are offered in the fun fair of life, and never starts on the quest for the goodly pearl of great price.

'*the vainglory of life*'. The word translated '*life*' here means 'one's style of living'. Its '*vainglory*' refers to the conceit and self-glorying of the braggart, his pompous air of superiority over his fellows. It is the habitual pose of the strutting ego. The politician who glories in his power to sway audiences, the business man who brags of what he pays in super-tax, the vain woman who boasts of her fashionable friends, the Robinsons who are determined to 'keep up with the Joneses', and the evangelist who boasts of his many converts, are all illustrations of '*the vainglory of life*'.

2^{17}. '*And the world passeth away*'; cf. 2^8. The world—this society which is dominated by the prince of evil and whose people and institutions oppose the will of the Eternal—is doomed to perish. The new Age of God has begun. Already Christ has overcome the Devil (see *Note 17*, p. 82) and broken his power; His dominion will increase as Satan's will decrease. John is thinking of the mighty Roman Empire; that 'Babylon the great' whose terrible destruction was foretold by the Seer of Patmos some years later (Rev. 17^5, etc.). The worldliness of Rome, which John now summarizes as '*the lust thereof*', is destroying the real life of its rulers and people, and its doom is inevitable. But John's words have a timeless significance. Through all the Christian centuries, the '*world*', with its defiant hostility to God, its materialistic ambitions, its superficial values, its pomp and pretensions, has been passing away. All that it stands for is only a transient phase of life, which is gradually being superseded by those Christian values and standards which show the extending sovereignty of the Eternal over human life. And surely a realistic view of modern life justifies John's statement. Despite the upsurge of great anti-Christian movements, some of which have already passed away, can we not say that an increasing number of people today have more Christian standards of behaviour, loftier conceptions of duty, and nobler enthusiasms for world brotherhood and peace than ever before?

The Christian who '*doeth the will of God*', who lives under the direction and by the power of Christ, is not only a citizen of this passing world; he belongs to the permanent order of God's people, and he '*abideth*' with God in the fellowship of that eternal life which goes on '*for ever*'.

(c) 2¹⁸⁻²⁸. The Test of True Believing

John concludes the section 1⁵-2²⁸ by giving the third test whereby the Christian can be assured that he is living the life of fellowship with God; the test of True Believing.

> **2¹⁸⁻²³. Summary:** *Your faith is now being tested. The fact that you live in a critical age is proved by the appearance of many antichrists; heretical teachers who actually deny the real divinity of Jesus, and so repudiate the God whom He revealed. 'The enlightened ones' they call themselves, but the light of the* true *knowledge of God is available for every simple believer.*

2¹⁸. John's readers have often '*heard*' from preachers that one day Antichrist would come to test their faith. Well, the time has now come; '*even now have there arisen many antichrists*'. On the meaning of Antichrist and John's description of the heretics as '*antichrists*', see *Note 13*, p. 67.

'*It is the last hour.*' Jesus certainly taught that a 'last day' would come when history would end and God's Kingdom would be finally established; but He plainly said that even He did not know its date (Mk 13³²) and told His disciples that it was none of their business (Acts 1⁷). What was central and distinctive in His teaching was His declaration that, when His ministry came to its climax in the Cross and the Resurrection, the sovereign Rule of God had already begun on earth. The long-expected Age to Come had *arrived* and those who believed in Him were already living in it. This was made even more clear in John's Gospel, where Jesus said again and again that 'eternal life', life in the Age to Come, can be experienced here and now, and that judgement on world evil is not postponed to the end of history, but is a present and continuous fact. And this is the main teaching of the apostles; a present

Saviour and a present Salvation. By the middle of the first century, however, many Jewish Christians, failing to realize how radically Jesus had reinterpreted current thought about 'the last things', centred their hopes in the *final* coming of God's Kingdom, and indeed eagerly looked for that coming and the end of history *in their own time*. In his Gospel, John's mind is largely dominated by the teaching of his master, the Apostle John, that Christ's distinctive message was that the Age to Come had already arrived. On the other hand, there is some evidence that he was not indifferent to the 'popular' interest in the final consummation of the Kingdom (*WFH*, pp. 106-28). After John 5$^{25-7}$, with its thought of a *present* resurrection and judgement, John adds verses 28-9 which refer to the *final* resurrection and judgement. In the same way, he adds 'and I will raise him up at the last day' in John 6$^{39, 40, 44, 54}$, and 'in the last day' in John 12^{48}, though these 'tags' seem at variance with the thought of the passages. In the verse we are studying, moved by the very critical situation of his day, John voices the popular (and mistaken) conviction that '*the last hour*' of history is about to strike.

Westcott and others have stressed the fact that the literal translation is, 'It is *a* last hour'. It is very doubtful if this is what John meant, but such a thought would have been nearer the truth, and more in line with the thought of Jesus. Our Lord said that there would be crises, some of them in the lifetime of His hearers, in which men would 'see the coming of God's Reign with power' (Mk 9^1, Moffatt; *CLM*, p. 68; and also comment on 2^{28} concerning the 'parousia'). Among these crises, He foretold the appearance of false Christs and false prophets (Mk 13$^{5-6, 21-3}$), and this prediction was being fulfilled in John's day. A crisis had arisen which was far more dangerous than the fall of Jerusalem, persecution by the Jews, or impending persecution by Domitian. For the first time, widespread heresy was massing its forces against the Christian faith and threatening its survival. This was one of the ultimate crises in the history of Christendom. It heralded the '*last hour*', not of the world's life, but *of an age*. The Church heeded the warning of such leaders as John, and in the next century triumphantly resisted the heresy of Gnosticism. In the following centuries, the Empire itself became nominally Christian and the great Creeds of the Church were formulated.

History itself consists of a series of critical periods in which civilizations rise and fall, and in the history of Christendom there have been many last hours and new beginnings. In a real sense, we today are living in such a last hour. Antichrist, in the form of a perilous drift away from Christianity and the widespread acceptance of secular and totalitarian ideologies, has brought mankind to an hour when its very existence may be threatened by complete atomic destruction. In the supreme crisis which Jesus called 'your hour and the power of darkness', He fought against the Prince of Evil and defeated him (Lk 22^{53}, Jn 12$^{23, 31}$, etc.). At the end of the century, the Church was empowered by Christ the Victor to withstand the attacks of the antichrists and triumph over them. Is the Church being prepared to meet the crisis of today? The massed forces of evil are dreadfully formidable and they cannot be defeated by merely human powers; hence the prevalent mood of 'quiet desperation'. But, if our faith in Christ is so strong that He can use us for His purposes, we may yet 'see the coming of God's Reign with power' in our own age.

2^{19}. *'They went out from us'*. For the first time, the Asian Church has to deal with organized heresy and a large-scale secession from its fellowship. On the general nature of the heresy, see p. 3; for fuller details, see comment on 2^{22} and *Note 14*, p. 68. We do not know the details of the heretics' break with the Church, but *'they went out'* suggests that they were not excommunicated, but that, failing to win the other leaders of the Church to their new theology, they deliberately seceded and formed their own 'Christian' society.

'they were not of us'; otherwise *'they would have continued with us'*. Their names have been on the Church roll, but their membership has never been more than nominal. The fact that they have left the fellowship shows that they never really belonged to it. As John has said (see comment on 1^{3}), it is when a man unreservedly commits himself to Christ as his divine Saviour that he becomes one with all others who share this common faith and this common participation in the divine life. But these heretics deny the very basis of the faith— the incarnation—and therefore they have never been in real fellowship with God through union with Christ. They have failed to meet the test, not only of right living and genuine loving, but also of true believing.

Why do people leave the Church today as casually as they

may resign from the Rotary Club or the Choral Society? Behind the trivial reasons they give is a failure in faith. Perhaps their 'conversion' was a matter of emotion only; perhaps their original commitment to Christ was a formal decision which was expected of them by devout parents; and perhaps the local church received them into membership before their faith in a divine Saviour and Lord was firmly established, and before they recognized the tremendous demands which Christ makes upon His disciples. If so, it is not surprising that they now leave the Church, the secret of whose fellowship they have never really understood or experienced.

'*that they might be made manifest*'; i.e. that it might be made plain (*RSV*).

'*that they all are not of us*'; i.e. that not one of them really belonged to the fellowship of the true Church. These heretics had been respected by the laity as inspired prophets, but it was now evident that they were not inspired by *God* (see comment on 4[1]). Even while they denied the basic truth of Christianity, they claimed to be Christians—indeed, Christians of a superior type—and now, as professing 'believers', they were carrying on a missionary campaign among the pagans which was meeting with considerable success (see comment on 4[5]). Perhaps some of the laity are disturbed by this news, and are wondering if the heresy ought not to have been tolerated in order that a secession might be avoided. No, says John, it was *providential* that they left us, 'that it might be made plain' that what they believe is a fundamental denial of the truth of the Christian gospel. The Church is not stronger but weaker, if, in the name of religious tolerance, its witness to the true faith is compromised for the sake of larger membership figures.

2[20]. '*an anointing*' (*RV*) or '*unction*' (*AV*) translates the Greek *chrisma* (cf. 'Christ' which means 'Anointed One'). In the Old Testament, the act of anointing was a ceremony in which priests, prophets and kings were consecrated to their high office.

'*ye have an anointing*'. The '*ye*' is emphatic and may be translated 'you too'. John is making a contrast between the heretics of 2[19] and 'you true believers'. C. H. Dodd thinks it probable that the heretics claimed to have received their superior knowledge of divine things in a special ceremony of 'anointing' or initiation, similar to that of the pagan mystery religions (*CHD*, p. 61). John says, *You too* have an anointing, but yours is a genuine anointing, for you have received it from '*the Holy One*'. This may refer to the Father. More probably, in view of the context and of Mark 1[24], John 6[69], Acts 3[14], and Revelation 3[7], it refers to Christ. In the Old Testament, it is said that those who were anointed to high office were given the gift of God's Spirit (e.g. 1 Sam 16[13], Isa 61[1]). At His baptism in the Jordan, when Jesus was consecrated to His saving ministry, He too, and in the fullest sense, received the Holy Spirit (Lk 3[22], 4[18], Jn 3[34], Acts 10[38]). So, after a glance forward to 2[27], we see that John is here saying to his readers, When, at your conversion, Christ consecrated you into His service, He gave you the gift of the Holy Spirit; and it is in virtue of this gift of the Spirit of Truth (Jn 14[17], 15[26]), who will guide you into all truth (Jn 16[13]), that

'*ye know all things*'. But this is not the best reading. The older MSS read '*you all know*' (*RSV*), and that surely is what John wrote. In the Old Testament, only selected people were anointed and given God's Spirit. The Asian heretics claimed that specially imparted knowledge of divine things was the privilege of their own select little coterie. On the contrary, writes John, the knowledge of these boastful 'knowers' is sheer delusion, but you *all* have knowledge; every one of you has received from Christ, through the Spirit of Truth, that true knowledge of God which is sufficient for your full salvation. Saving knowledge is the privilege, not of the cultured few, but of every genuine member of the Church (see further in *Note 8*, p. 43).

2[21]. John's meaning is something like this: 'I am not writing to tell you how you may know God. As I have just said, you already have that knowledge. I am writing to remind you that any so-called 'knowledge' of God which may bear a superficial resemblance to the truth you possess, but which is actually a flat denial of it, is just a plain lie, to be exposed and uncompromisingly repudiated'. On '*the truth*', see *Note 4*, p. 25.

2[22]. '*Who is the liar?*' Who is the supreme liar, '*the antichrist*'? Of course, John's readers know that he is referring to the heretics, whom he has already described as '*many antichrists*' in 2[18] (see *Note 13*, p. 67). But now, at last, John defines the supreme lie which, if it were not refuted, would imperil the very survival of the Christian faith. This dangerous antichrist is '*he that denieth that Jesus is the Christ*'. The Incarnation is the basic fact upon which Christianity is grounded. John makes that clear, not only here but also in 3^{23}, $4^{2, 15}$, $5^{1, 5, 20}$. Why is this doctrine of supreme importance to the Christian? Why and how did the Asian heretics deny it? Is there a modern form of this denial of the Incarnation? These questions are discussed in *Note 14*, p. 68.

'*denieth*'. The verb 'to deny' is used in two senses in the New Testament: to reject a revealed truth (cf. 1 Tim 5^8); or to *disown* a person, as when Jesus said that every would-be disciple must 'deny himself' (Mk 8^{34}), and when He warned Peter that he would deny Him (Mk 14^{30}). Here 'to deny' means to reject the basic truth that Jesus is the Son of God, but such a denial inevitably leads to the more fundamental denial; the disowning of Christ as the divine Saviour. Jesus Himself has warned us that this is man's most deadly sin (see Mt 10^{33}; cf. Mk 8^{38}, Acts 3^{13-4}).

'*denieth the Father*'. Because of their denial of the truth of Christ's claim that 'he that hath seen me hath seen the Father' (Jn 14^9), the heretics have a conception of the character of God which is full of error (cf. Mt 11^{27}, Jn 12^{44-5}). He is a stranger to them; an 'unknown God'; 'Absolute Being', 'Eternal Reason', or some other vague philosophical abstraction (see *Note 8*, p. 43).

2^{23}. '*hath not the Father*'. Jesus said, 'No one cometh unto the Father, but by me' (Jn 14^6). It is only as we have faith-union with the divine Son that we can 'have' (possess, enter into joyous experience of) of the divine Father (see *Note 10*, p. 48).

'*confesseth*'. John has already spoken of the confession of sins (1^9). Here, as in $4^{2, 15}$, he speaks of confessing Jesus as the Christ, the Son of God. Confession is the direct opposite to *denial* (see here and Mt 10^{32-3}, Jn 1^{20}), and 'confess', like 'deny' (see comment on 2^{22}), has a double meaning. (1) It may mean to acknowledge or declare a *fact*. So John writes about confessing that Jesus is the Son of God ($4^{2, 15}$; cf. Jn 12^{42}, Phil. 2^{11}). In this sense, we speak of the declaration that 'Thou art the Christ' (Mk 8^{29}) as Peter's 'confession'. In John's insistence on a true confession of facts about Jesus, we see the beginning of that formulation of orthodoxy which issued, in a later age, in the great Creeds of the Church. (2) But to 'confess' may also mean to acknowledge and declare adherence to a *person*, as in this verse and in 4³, Jn 9²², Rom 10⁹. We must not over-stress this distinction. The man who declares, as a matter of strong conviction, that Jesus is the Son of God must, almost inevitably, commit himself to Christ as his divine Saviour, and so 'confess' Christ in the fullest sense of the word. It is this intelligent and public confession that our Lord requires of every one of us; if we openly confess Him before men, He will openly acknowledge us as His true disciples in the presence of God (Mt 10³²⁻³). He calls us to make 'the good confession in the sight of many witnesses' (1 Tim 6¹²), declaring our commitment to our Saviour in word and deed, and undeterred by what His enemies may threaten to do to us (cf. Jn 9²²). 'With 'confess that' and 'confess', compare the distinction between 'believe that' and 'believe in'; see *Note 18*, p. 90.

NOTE 13. ANTICHRIST AND ANTICHRISTS

The word '*Antichrist*' has a double meaning. It can mean one who takes the place of the Christ, a mock-Christ whose policy is one of satanic deception; it can also mean one who opposes Christ and is His deadly enemy. The actual name 'Antichrist' appears in *1 and 2 John* for the first time in extant literature (2¹⁸, ²², 4³, 2 Jn 7), but the legend of this dread personality, under one name or another, had been popular among the Jews since the publication of *Daniel* (c. 167 B.C.). It was believed that, before history ended with the final intervention of God, the powers of evil, concentrated in the person of a supreme monster of iniquity, would make one last desperate attack upon God's people. When the mad Emperor Caligula, claiming to be a god, tried to erect a statue of himself in the Jerusalem Temple just before his death in A.D. 40, many Jews thought that *he* was the dreaded Antichrist, and it was about this time that many Christians adopted this Jewish belief. Was not Jesus reported to have said, 'When ye see the abomination of desolation standing where he ought not . . .' (Mk 13¹⁴), and did not this refer to the coming of the Antichrist? In one of his earlier letters, Paul seems to feel that the blasphemous self-deification which had shown itself in Caligula would come to a dreadful climax in a future emperor. He does not call him Antichrist, but 'the man of sin . . . that opposeth himself and exalteth himself' against God (2 Thess 2³⁻⁴). The author of the *Apocalypse* saw Antichrist in the person of Emperor Domitian (the 'beast') and the cult of emperor-worship (the 'second beast') and foretold that the final conflict between Christ and Antichrist was at hand.

John, however, not only abandons all the grotesque imagery of the popular Antichrist legend, but almost completely ignores the critical political events of his day. The great conflict which will finally bring an end to history will not be in the realm of politics, but of *ideas*. The Antichrist will bring all heresy to its climax in a last desperate attempt to destroy the Christian faith and inaugurate a world-wide apostasy. Meanwhile, the Church faces an immediate crisis. The prophecy of Jesus, 'For there shall arise false Christs and false prophets . . . that they may lead astray, if possible the elect' (Mk 13^{22}) was for the first time being fulfilled. '*Even now have there arisen many antichrists*' (2^{18}) who are the forerunners of the supreme Antichrist; false prophets who are inspired by the Evil One to deny the very foundations of the true faith (2^{22}, 4^3, 2 Jn 7). They are not mock-Christs, satanic caricatures of the Son of God, but they are deadly enemies of Christ and His Church. They are masquerading as the true interpreters of Christianity, and by their plausible heresies and high-sounding pretensions they are deceiving some of the faithful (2 Jn 7) and seducing them into apostasy. Antichrists, indeed! (See comment on 2^{22} and *Note 14*, p. 68.) John endorses Paul's conviction that 'We wrestle not against flesh and blood, but against . . . spiritual hosts of wickedness' (Eph 6^{12}).

Let us heed John's warning today. 'The supreme enemy of Christ's redeeming work is radically false belief' (*CHD*, p. 50). Nothing is so powerful as a firmly held idea, and nothing is so diabolical and dangerous as the power of a wrong idea firmly held and fervently proclaimed. Never has this been more obvious than in modern history. Think of the false ideologies of today—the ideologies of secular humanism, atheistic communism, political totalitarianism, racial exclusiveness; these are the antichrists which are the monstrous enemies of Christ and His cause. It is against these dread heresies that the Church must be belligerently aggressive. During the past fifty years, in the matter of the propagation of the true faith, the Church has all too often been the Church Apologetic rather than the Church Aggressive, the Church Inoffensive rather than the Church Militant. In the critical years in which we live and preach, the issue is still between reality and illusion, belief and unbelief, love and hate, Christianity and apostasy. The only hope for the world is the victory of our faith (5^4; see *Note 25*, p. 114).

NOTE 14. THE PERSON OF JESUS CHRIST

The question Jesus put to the disciples, 'Whom say ye that I am?', is the fundamental question which He puts to every generation of men. John's first answer, '*Jesus is the Christ*' (2^{22}; cf. 5^1) reproduces the answer of Peter in Mark 8^{29}, but this meant far more to the early Church than that Jesus was the Messiah of the Jews. Matthew made this clear when he interpreted Peter's confession by enlarging

it into 'Thou art the Christ, the Son of the living God' (Mt 16¹⁶).
Compare with this what seems to have been the earliest creed of the
Church; 'Jesus Christ is Lord' (Rom 10⁹, Phil 2¹¹, Acts 16³¹). It is
this truth, that Jesus was both Son of Man and Son of God, truly
human and truly divine, which dominates John's Gospel from John
1¹, ¹⁴ onwards, and which, in this Epistle, he emphasizes when he
calls Jesus the '*Son of God*' (3²³, 4¹⁵, 5¹⁰, ¹³, ²⁰) and when he underlines the fact that '*Jesus Christ is come in the flesh*' (4²; cf. 1¹⁻³).
John was affirming the basic doctrine of Christianity, that of the
Incarnation. How could God ever be perfectly known, except by
One who had been 'in the bosom of the Father' (Jn 1¹⁸) from all
eternity? And how could such a One bring that revelation of the
character of God to men, except by descending into their midst and
living it out in a real human life?

In one way or another, the heretics of John's day were denying the
possibility and the fact of the Incarnation, because of their Gnostic
assumption that matter is essentially evil, and that therefore God
cannot possibly make any sort of contact with the material world
(see p. 5). This denial of the Incarnation landed them into Docetism
(from the Greek verb 'to seem'). The Docetists accepted the divinity,
but denied the humanity of Jesus. They held that He only *seemed* to
have a human body. Actually He was a sort of phantom, without
real flesh or blood. They said that He left no footprints on the
ground, for his body had neither substance nor weight. He only
seemed to die on the Cross. The human life of the celestial Christ
was a sort of divine play-acting, in which was lived out that divine
revelation of the truth whose meaning could be fathomed only by
those specially equipped to interpret it.

A special form of this theory was held by those who followed
Cerinthus, a gnostic heretic who, according to tradition, was John's
chief opponent. The story of John and Cerinthus in the public baths
at Ephesus is well known, and Irenaeus said that John wrote his
Gospel to refute Cerinthus. He held that the human Jesus and the
heavenly Christ were two quite separate persons. Jesus was the
human son of Joseph and Mary. Christ was a heavenly spirit or
aeon, who descended upon the man Jesus at His baptism and continued with Him throughout His ministry, using Him as a medium
of divine revelation. The truths taught were Christ's, but the voice
which spoke them was the voice of Jesus. When Christ had completed His message to mankind, after Gethsemane but before
Calvary, He left the man Jesus and returned to heaven. He who
suffered the humiliation and agony of the Cross was the human
Jesus, not the celestial Christ. The Cross had no saving significance
for them, nor any challenge.

It was such basic denials of the Incarnation that John attacked
throughout this letter, and we as preachers must expose and refute
any modern form of this heresy. Today the heresy usually takes the

F

reverse form of accepting the humanity, but denying the divinity of Jesus Christ; but to deny either the humanity or the divinity is to deny the Incarnation. That Jesus was very man *and* very God, as a matter of theological explanation, is an insoluble mystery, but, as a matter of historical fact and religious experience, we must affirm it as a glorious certainty.

Some Christians today reject the idea that the knowledge and power of Jesus were genuinely those of a man. But if Jesus was not really a man, but was only God pretending to be man, (i) God came part of the way into human life to save us, but not the whole way. We can no longer say, as a modern Christian has said, 'The God who could not capture my heart as He sat on a throne, overwhelmed me for ever when He cried in a cradle and died on a Cross'. (ii) Jesus cannot be our example of perfect manhood. Unlike us, He was never baffled by life's mysteries. He was never really tempted or lonely. Even His tears and His prayers were play-acting. Gethsemane was not a real agony, and there was no pain or passion in the spectacle of the Cross. (iii) He is not really our Saviour. It was not as our Representative that He offered the perfect sacrifice on our behalf, that our sins might be forgiven (see comment on 2^2). If He was only our kinsman in name, He could not offer anything on our behalf, for He was never really one of us. And He cannot be the Head of a new humanity, for He was never human.

Some Christians, and the majority of our contemporaries, accept the humanity of Jesus, but deny His real divinity. At best, if they are non-Christians, they regard Him as the noblest teacher the world has known. If they are professing Christians, they argue that all men are sons of God (which is not true), but that Jesus was the perfect son of God; that the difference between Him and us is one of degree. Just as God inspired the ancient prophets, so in a fuller sense He inspired Jesus to know and do His will, and this was possible because Jesus was perfectly receptive to God's self-revelation. So Jesus interpreted the nature and will of God to us, as no other had ever done; in this sense, Jesus has the 'value' of God for us. But, if Jesus was not really God-incarnate, then Christianity is no longer a supernatural religion which proclaims a supernatural salvation. We can no longer sing, 'Glory to God in the highest', in that He condescended to become one of us that He might redeem all of us. When Christ died on the Cross, sin was exposed as the destruction of the noblest of men; it was not seen in all its enormity as an attempt to destroy God Himself. What brought Jesus to Calvary was the heroic loyalty of a great prophet to the cause of truth and world reform; it was not the infinite, redemptive love of God, and we can no longer sing,

> *Amazing love! how can it be*
> *That Thou, my God, shouldst die for me!* (*MHB* 371)

It follows, also, that the story of the resurrection is a legend. Jesus had no right to say 'Lo, I am with you alway', and our claim to have a present, intimate experience of the living Christ is sheer imagination.

In answer to Philip's question, Jesus said, 'He that hath seen me hath seen the Father' (Jn 14⁹), and Dorothy Sayers described that as 'the most staggering reply ever heard by human ears'. But, staggering though it be, we must accept it as gospel truth; we must hold fast to the declaration of the Apostles' Creed: 'I believe . . . in Jesus Christ His only Son our Lord, who was . . . born of the Virgin Mary, suffered under Pontius Pilate, was crucified, dead and buried'. With conviction we must sing,

> *He deigns in flesh to appear,*
>   *Widest extremes to join;*
> *To bring our vileness near,*
>   *And make us all divine:*
> *And we the life of God shall know,*
> *For God is manifest below.* (*MHB* 142)

2²⁴⁻⁸. Summary: *Maintain your loyalty to the original gospel under the guidance of the Spirit, and so remain in union with Christ and the Father and possess eternal life. Then, steadfast in the truth, you will have confidence in the presence of Christ.*

2²⁴. '*As for you*', in contrast with the antichrists, '*let that abide with you which ye heard from the beginning*'. The gospel has been preached to them by John and others from the very beginning of their Christian life. John urges them to let its fundamental truths have a permanent home in their hearts, so that no plausible heresy will ever disturb their faith in Christ, or break the intimacy of their union with '*the Son*' and '*the Father*' (see comment on 2²³, and *Note 10*, p. 48). Whenever the clever arguments of the 'enlightened' or the sceptic—or the shattering blows of misfortune, the lure of worldliness, the deadening monotony of the common task—threaten to make us loosen our hold on Christ and lose the thrill of eternal life in union with Him, then let us turn back to 'the old, old story of Jesus and His love', and rediscover our Saviour and the wonder of daily fellowship with Him.

2²⁵. '*life eternal*'. See *Note 2*, p. 17.

2²⁶. '*These things*' refers especially to 2¹⁸⁻²⁵.

'*would lead you astray*'—but they need not succeed, as John shows in 2²⁷.

2²⁷. John tells his readers that the promise of the heretics to give them a fuller knowledge of God by teaching them a higher form of Christianity is both false and superfluous. Already they have everything they need. As he has just reminded them (see comment on 2²⁴), the gospel has been faithfully preached to them and is now their permanent possession. But more; as he has said in 2²⁰, when they became Christians, Christ gave them the gift of the Spirit, and He is the Spirit of Truth who will expose all heresy, for there '*is no lie*' in Him. He '*abideth*' in them, and He will ever remind them of the basic truths of the gospel (Jn 14²⁶), guide them into a growing understanding of those truths (Jn 16¹³) and show them how to apply them in every situation. And the supreme truth He teaches is that, by simple and sincere faith, the Christian may 'abide in' Christ (see *Note 10*, p. 48). Such a word should rebuke that note of diffidence and uncertainty which so often obtrudes itself into our preaching. Imagine a preacher saying, 'This question is very difficult, and perhaps we shall never find a quite satisfactory answer to it, but may we suggest that the gospel of Christ gives some sort of an answer, though we must admit that, in doing so, it raises a lot of other difficult questions?' John would have nothing to do with such apologetic dilly-dallying. Christ gives the answer to every legitimate question, if we can understand it. We find His answer in the gospel, and His indwelling Spirit will interpret that answer to us, and show us how to apply it to every life-situation.

2²⁸. '*abide in him*'. Taking the phrase from the previous verse, John urges his '*little children*' to maintain their spiritual union with Christ, and stresses one particular motive for doing so.

'*at his coming*'. Before we study the whole verse, we must ask what John means by this phrase. Those Christians who believed that God was about to make His final intervention into history (see comment on 2¹⁸) naturally concluded that Christ's final advent would take place at the same time. They used the Greek noun '*parousia*' (=arrival, visitation) of this final coming. But the word '*parousia*' is found in only one of the Gospels—that of Matthew—and in each case it is an editorial addition to his sources (cf. Mt 24³ with Mk 13⁴, and Mt 24²⁷, ³⁷, ³⁹ with Lk 17²⁴, ²⁶⁻⁷). Matthew's tendency to encourage the immediate-visible-advent hope is also found in Matthew 16²⁸ (cf. Mk 9¹). Indeed, in my judgement, none of the genuine sayings of Jesus about a 'coming again' foretold a *visible* and *final* return to earth in the immediate future. In John's Gospel, however, Jesus thinks of the coming of the Holy Spirit, His *alter ego*, as a spiritual coming-again of Himself into world life. We see this when we read consecutively such verses as John $14^{16, 18, 20, 28}$, $16^{7, 16}$ (see *Note 20*, p. 96). Jesus also thought of the coming fall of Jerusalem as a spiritual coming-again of Himself, this time in judgement (i.e. see Lk 17^{24-32}, Jn 16^{11}). It seems, therefore, that Jesus not only envisaged a series of crises in the future of the Kingdom (see p. 62), but that He thought of these crises as events in which He Himself, in the person of the Holy Spirit, would come again in mighty power into world life.

John uses the word '*parousia*' only once, in this verse. If he foretells the end of history in 2^{18}, he must be referring to the visible coming of Christ at the end of history in 2^{28}. This is confirmed by the fact that '*if he shall be manifested*' recurs in 3^2, where it obviously refers to the final *parousia*. The reading '*if*' (*RV*) is found in the best MSS and is to be preferred to '*when*' (*AV, RSV*); and this '*if*' is significant. John does not mean that the final advent may never come, but he does not attempt to put a date to it. We might translate, 'whenever he shall be manifested, whether in the near or distant future'.

'*boldness*'. The word recurs in 3^{21}, 4^{17}, 5^{14}. Literally it means 'frankness of speech', but its general meaning is 'confidence', or, to quote a helpful paraphrase, 'glad fearlessness of bearing'. If we '*abide in*' Christ, we shall look forward to His final advent, not with dismay, but with joyous confidence. See also comments on 3^{21}, 4^{17}.

'*ashamed*'. Jesus said, 'Whosoever shall be ashamed of me . . . the Son of man also shall be ashamed of him, when he cometh in the glory of the Father' (Mk 8^{38}). In that day, if our confession of Christ has been a merely formal one, we shall be utterly '*ashamed*' to hear Him say, 'I never knew you' (Mt 7^{23}). Only if, in a lifetime of deepening devotion, we '*abide in him*' shall we be able to look forward with any confidence to hear Him say, 'Come, ye blessed of my Father' (Mt 25^{34}).

The preacher is justified in giving a wider interpretation to this verse, and one, I think, in harmony with the mind of Jesus. Every age in which secularism and anti-Christian ideologies defy the sovereignty of Christ, scorn His saviourhood, and seek to bring in another dark age of unbelief and apostasy, is an age in which Christ may 'come again' into world life in spiritual power and triumph, to overthrow the hosts of heresy and inaugurate a new age of faith. In such an age we live. In such an age Christ may 'come again'. Whether, if He comes, He will be able to use us to further His purposes will depend on the answer to His question, 'Howbeit when the Son of man cometh, shall he find faith on the earth' (Lk 18[8])? He bids us prepare a highway for His advent by our faith and devotion, being ever on the alert, for His comings are often sudden and unexpected (Mk 13[33, 36]). Like G. K. Chesterton, we must pray, 'From sleep and damnation, deliver us, good Lord'. If, in this age of crisis, we '*abide in him*', we shall be able to meet Him with 'glad fearlessness of hearing' and unashamed. Further, we shall be able to witness for Him with a like confidence. When we have to face the hostility, the persecution, the ridicule of modern antichrists, we shall not be flustered or fearful. We shall have that joyous confidence in the power of our indwelling Saviour which marked the lives of so many of the early Christians (see Mk 13[11], Acts 4[13], 16[25], 2 Cor 3[12], 1 Tim 3[13]).

(B) 2[29]-4[6]. THE CHRISTIAN LIFE IS LIFE IN THE FAMILY OF GOD.

This is the second main section of the Epistle, and again John applies the tests of Right Living, Genuine Loving, and True Believing.

(a) 2[29]-3[10]. The Test of Right Living

2[29]-3[3]. Summary: *Right living is evidence that we have been born into God's family. 'God's Children'; what a privilege, and how it reveals His love for us. But that is not all; one day we shall be like Christ Himself. Therefore let us strive after His perfection.*

2[29]. This transitional verse is really linked with 3[1-3].

'*If* [i.e. Because] *ye know that he* [i.e. God] *is righteous*' (see comment on 1[9]). John is summarizing the argument of 1[5]-2[6], that right living is a test of our fellowship with God and of abiding in Christ. Here he says that by this same test we can know that we are '*begotten of him*' (i.e. God). See *Note 15*, p. 77.

3¹. On God's love for us, which is also stressed in **4⁹⁻¹⁰, ¹⁶, ¹⁹**, see *Note 16*, p. 79. In this verse, *'us'* and *'we'* refer to all true believers, in contrast to the heretics who falsely claim to be uniquely related to God.

'children of God'. It is generally believed, today, that every man and woman is by nature a child of God and has the right to call God 'My Father'. This was also a common opinion in the first century. Paul quoted Aratus, the Stoic poet, as saying, 'We are also his offspring' (Acts 17²⁸), and when John wrote many Hellenists held that the spiritual part of man's being is an offspring of, or emanation from, God. This is not Christian doctrine. When the prodigal 'son' came to himself in the far country, he realized that he had never really been a son. It was not till he returned home, and entered into a true filial relationship with his father, that he became a real 'son'. Just so, God has created us, and in His own 'image'; that is, He has given us biological life and the potentiality of spiritual life. But, until that potentiality is realized, we are His *creatures*, but not yet His *children*. Jesus told us to love our enemies, not because we *are*, but that we *may be* the sons of our Father (Mt 5⁴⁵), and when hostile Jews boasted that God was their Father, Jesus denied their claim (Jn 8⁴¹, ⁴⁴). It is not by nature, but by grace, that we become *'children of God'*, and the one condition is that we believe in Jesus Christ (Jn 1¹²). But, as John has already said (see *Note 6*, p. 36), although believers are expected not to sin, in fact their mastery over sin is far from complete. They are still sinners—and yet they are *'called children of God'* and by God Himself. What a privilege this is, and utterly undeserved. How wonderful is God's love for us that He gives us this filial status, says John.

'and such we are' (*RV*). Some inferior MSS omit this phrase, as also does *AV*; but it is authentic and important. C. H. Spurgeon's sermon on 'And such we are' has as its title, 'A Jewel from the Revised Version'. We who are 'in Christ' are not only 'adopted' by God and given the status of sons (Rom 8¹⁴⁻¹⁷); we are not only *'called'* His children; we actually *are* the children of God. We have been born again, this time in a spiritual sense (see *Note 15*, p. 77). God, who created us, has now *'begotten'* us, and we actually have begun to share in His nature and life. We are, we really are, His children. There is breathless wonder in the phrase. It's quite incredible, but it's an amazing fact.

'*the world*'. See *Note 7*, p. 38.

'*knoweth us not*'. The world never recognized Jesus for what He was, the unique Son of God; they saw only the small town carpenter, the itinerant preacher, the crucified idealist. Then how can we expect worldlings to understand *us*, who are beginning to share His supernatural nature? They will always be puzzled by us, regarding us as queer people, and hating us for what they regard as our superior airs and crazy claims. If the worldling is *not* puzzled by us, there is something wrong with our life and witness.

3². '*now . . . not yet*'. The Christian must not only glory in a present experience; he must eagerly stretch forward to the future. The man who says, 'I am a saved man; I have been born again and am a child of God', may be speaking of a starting-point as if it were a terminus. He rejoices in the 'Now', but ignores the 'Not yet', and that is the way to spiritual drudgery and mediocrity. We are saved, but not yet fully saved. We possess eternal life *now*, but *not yet* in its fullness. '*Now are we children of God*', but the wonder of '*what we shall be*' is '*not yet*'.

'*we know that*'. On Christian Certainty, see *Note 27*, p. 124.

'*if he shall be manifested*' could be translated 'if *it* (i.e. our future glory) shall be manifested'. In either case, '*if*' means 'whenever'; see comment on 2²⁸.

The second half of this verse can be translated in two ways (*CHD*, p. 71), and each expresses a truth. Perhaps John was intentionally ambiguous. (*a*) It can mean, 'We know that we shall be *like* Christ, because we shall *see* Him as He really is, and only like can see like' (cf. Mt 5⁸). (*b*) But John probably had in mind the alternative meaning: 'Because we shall *see* Christ in the glory of His real nature, we shall, we know, become *like* Him—for our vision of Him as He *is* will transform us into *what* He is.' Those who *saw* the human Jesus with understanding eyes and heart were transformed into new people, and became *like* Him in some degree. Think of that strange little medley of disciples which became 'the glorious company of the Apostles'. Just so, in our own experience, we are transfigured by our 'vision' of Christ in all the glory of His revealing and saving love (see 2 Cor 3¹⁸, Rom 8²⁹). But then —see (*a*) above—as we become more *like* Christ, we *see* Him with deeper understanding, and in turn this fuller vision makes us more *like* Him—and so the blessed process continues. But the glory of the Incarnate Son was confined within the limits of a human life, so that even His most intimate disciples could never see Him in His true nature; and this is true of our 'vision', of Christ. But when He is 'manifested' at the end of history in all the fullness of His being, then we shall see Him as He really is, and that perfect vision will complete the work of transfiguration and make us even like Him. There is much that we do not know about the hereafter, but do we want to know anything more wonderful than this? (On man's vision of God, see comment on 4¹².)

3³. *'purifieth himself'*. The glorious *'hope'* of **3²** must be a constant incentive to holier living. Daily the Christian must strive towards likeness to Christ by imitating the perfect holiness of Jesus (see **2⁶**). Among the defilements of the world, he must keep himself 'pure in heart' (Mt 5⁸, 1 Tim 5²²), lest any impurity of thought should cloud that vision of Christ which is transforming him (see comment on **3²**). His life must be one of constant ethical and spiritual progress. But *'purifieth himself'* needs some qualification. We must beware of the peril of self-sanctification. We cannot improve ourselves; that would be to rely on self instead of on Christ, and such self-centredness is sin. As John has said, it is the indwelling Christ who 'cleanseth us from all sin' (see comment on **1⁷ᵇ**). Our prayer must be, 'Lord, we beseech Thee, grant Thy people *grace* to withstand the temptations of the world, the flesh, and the devil, and with pure hearts and minds to follow Thee the only true God' (Collect for 18th Sunday after Trinity).

NOTE 15. BORN OF GOD

In **3¹**, John says that God, of His love, has not only changed our relationship to Him, so that we are *'called children of God'*; He has radically transformed us, so that *'we are'* His children in nature as well as in name, for we are *'begotten of him'* (**2²⁹**). The idea of salvation through regeneration was not unknown among the Hellenists, but John's thought is based on that of Jesus. Our Lord said, 'Whosoever shall not receive the kingdom of God as a little child, he shall in no wise enter therein' (Mk 10¹⁵). He said to Nicodemus, 'Except a man be born anew (and from above), he cannot see the kingdom of God' (Jn 3³). Using Johannine terminology, both verses mean, 'The only way to possess eternal life is to be born all over again—this time in a spiritual birth—and again to become a little child—but this time, a child of God'. This is the radical change which a man experiences at his conversion; the natural man becomes a spiritual man; from mere existence, he enters into real life; already born in time, he is now born into eternity (cf. 1 Pet 1²³). *Every* man must pass through some experience of re-birth, before he can claim to be a Christian. The refined people of Wesley's day were offended and felt themselves insulted by his insistence on this universal necessity, and the Duchess of Buckingham wrote to the Countess of Huntingdon that such doctrines were 'most repulsive and strongly tinctured with impertinence and disrespect towards their superiors'. In our own time, the word 'conversion' is not popular among those church-goers who argue that we can be *educated* into Christianity, and trained to apply its principles to the problems of daily conduct, and that that is enough. Dr J. E. Rattenbury has told us that, in a private conversation, Dr W. Russell Maltby once asked him: 'Are we teaching our people the need of a religious life deeper than that of the Wesleys *before* their conversion?' Every preacher should feel the challenge of that question.

How the new birth happens is a divine miracle and therefore, as Jesus told Nicodemus, it is a mystery. We shall never fully understand the psychology of conversion. But the new birth does not have to be understood before it can be experienced, any more than we have to be meteorological experts before we can feel the wind on our faces (cf. Jn 3⁷⁻⁸). And this supernatural miracle is a flat denial of that foolish catchphrase that 'you can't change human nature'. When G. Bernard Shaw said that 'once a man is born, it's too late to save him or damn him', G. K. Chesterton replied, 'That is the last lie in hell'.

Who are 'begotten' of God? John says, '*Whosoever believeth that Jesus is the Christ* (and commits himself to him) *is begotten of God*' (5¹; cf. John 1¹²). Accept Christ as your Saviour, enthrone Him as Lord at the centre of your being, and in His own mysterious way He will transform your life from the centre outwards. He will re-create your whole being, so that while, in a sense, you are still the same person, in a deeper sense you will become a very different person. This does not mean that your old self will be *reformed* and your old life will be enriched and deepened; it means that you will be re-born and begin to live an altogether different sort of life, which is a very sharing of God's life. Think, for instance, of the radical change that took place in Saul Kane, in John Masefield's *Everlasting Mercy*. (See also 2 Cor 5¹⁷, Gal 6¹⁵, Rom 6⁴, 2 Cor 4¹⁶.) And, as Jesus told Nicodemus, a man is never too old to have this experience. In Charles Morgan's *The Judge's Story*, the judge says: 'Is any man too old to accept, with joyous equanimity, a revolution in his life? Then he is already dead. Is he too stubborn and fearful to be re-born? Then he is a dummy of the armchair.'

In this Epistle, and apart from **5¹** (above), John concentrates on the *consequences* of the new birth. He who is born of God '*doeth righteousness*' (**2²⁹**). He '*doeth no sin*', indeed '*cannot sin*' (**3⁹**; **5¹⁸**; see *Note 6*, p. 36). He '*loveth*' both God and fellow man (**4⁷**; see *Note 9*, p. 45, and *Note 11*, p. 52). He '*overcometh the world*' (see *Note 25*, p. 114). He begins a new sort of life whose standard of behaviour is as high as perfection, and whose 'cost-of-living index' always rises and never falls. But his triumph over sin is not complete when he is first born of God; the process of regeneration lasts a lifetime, and he will constantly need to be 're-converted'. On this aspect of the new birth, see *Note 22*, p. 102.

NOTE 16. GOD'S LOVE FOR US

On the meaning of '*agapē*', see *Note 9*, p. 45, where also it is stressed that man's love for God is always 'caused', in the sense that '*We love, because he first loved us*' (**4¹⁹**). By contrast, God's love for man is spontaneous and uncaused. It is not a response to what is of worth in man, to something in man which makes him lovable. This is the wonder of it, that God loved us 'while we were yet sinners' (Rom 5⁸); while we were at our worst, not our best; while we were hating Him and were absorbed in our unlovely self-conceits. His is 'love to the loveless shown'. He loved us, not because we were worth loving—not because, behind our sordid egoism, our nasty habits, our grubby ambitions, our defiant hostility, He found something slightly attractive—but because '*God is love*' (**4⁸, ¹⁶**; see further in *Note 21*, p. 99). It is His nature to love.

His is a self-giving love which expressed itself, at infinite cost, in the Incarnation. '*Herein was the love of God manifested in us, that God hath sent his only begotten Son into the world*' (**4⁹**). 'God so loved the world that he gave' Himself to us in the person of 'his only begotten Son' (Jn 3¹⁶)—and every deed of the human Jesus revealed the wonder of that love. See Him, with His arms round little children, telling them unforgettable stories. See Him laying His hand on a loathsome leper, deliberately touching an untouchable to show him that he was not beyond the reach of God. See Him looking down with compassion on a harlot who is bathing His feet with tears of gratitude for what He has done for her. And so the story goes on . . . and he who has seen Jesus has seen God. This is how God loves; this is divine love in action. But the self-giving of the Incarnation came to its supreme, sacrificial expression in Gethsemane and the Cross. '*Hereby know we love, because he laid down his life for us*' (**3¹⁶**). He loves us that much.

> *Throughout the world its breath is known,*
> *Wide as infinity;*
> *So wide it never passed by one,*
> *Or it had passed by me.* (*MHB* 77)

But is it not true that Jesus had a very special love for 'the beloved disciple' (Jn 13²³, 21²⁰), for the rest of the Twelve (Jn 13¹, 14²¹), and for the family at Bethany? Is it true, therefore, as A. J. Gossip has said, that God 'has a particular affection for those who love Jesus Christ and all for which Christ stands' (*Interpreter's Bible* (8), p. 739)? This suggests that God loves the saint more than He loves the sinner; but His love for all men is an infinite love, and there is nothing greater than infinitude. Perhaps it would be more true to say that God is able to *express* His love more fully, and so to give Himself in richer measure, to those who respond to His love in gratitude and devotion.

We must not forget that the spontaneous, self-giving love of God is also an inexorable and, in a sense, a possessive love. He had made us to become His children, and, that He may win our hearts and possess us as His own, He pursues us with that tireless urgency which Francis Thompson has described in *The Hound of Heaven*. When we abandon our flight from Him and surrender to the claims of His love, then—amazing love—He calls us His '*children*' (see comment on 3¹). But He is not content with that. At all costs to Himself and to us, He will now *make* us His children in fact as well as in name. His inexorable purpose never flags. Because He loves us while we are still unlovable, He will never be satisfied until He has made us completely lovable. He insists on our complete devotion and obedience, because only thus can we become our finest selves and know the glory of eternal life.

3⁴⁻¹⁰. Summary: *Every form of sin is a rejection of Christ, who came to abolish sins and give us mastery over them. Let no clever arguments blind you to the fact that the children of the Devil continue in sin, but that the children of God must have done with it.*

3⁴. In contrast to the '*every one*' of 3³, John says that '*every one*' who claims that, because he is a specially enlightened sort of Christian, he is not bound to obey the moral laws which are binding on ordinary Christians, is a plain rebel against God. The man who says, 'I know God', and in the same breath says, 'I need not love my brother man'—the man who claims to be religious, but refuses to be ethical or to fulfil his social obligations—is just a plain sinner, whatever he calls himself.

'*lawlessness*'; see *Note 5*, p. 35.

3⁵. '*ye know that*'. On Christian Certainty, see *Note 27*, p. 124.
'*to take away sins*'. The Sinless One came to '*take away*' (i.e. abolish or destroy) not only 'the sin of the world' (Jn 1²⁹),

but every expression of it—the '*sins*' of thought, word and deed. So, to go on sinning is to nullify the whole purpose of the Incarnation. John reminds his readers that they already '*know*' the basic truth of the gospel of salvation; cf. Paul's similar statement in 1 Corinthians 15³. He does not here *expand* the doctrine of the Atonement, though such verses as 3⁵, 1⁷ᵇ, 2², 3⁸ᵇ provide the basis of such an exposition. In his preaching and teaching in the Ephesus district he has doubtless explained *how* Christ had abolished the sins of men. Have we laboured to do the same for our congregations? The preacher who takes 3⁵ for his text may safely take it for granted that most of his hearers are rather vague as to this '*How?*'.

3⁶. If Christ came for the express purpose of abolishing sin, the man who '*abideth in him*' (see *Note 10*, p. 48) must once and for all dissociate himself from every form of it (see *Note 6*, p. 36). If he goes on sinning, he is not a genuine Christian. He has never really been 'in Christ'; he has never really 'seen' Him (see comment on 3²) or had real intimacy with Him.

3⁷. Don't be deceived by plausible arguments. Human '*righteousness*' means more than 'being right with God' (as in Rom 4⁵⁻⁶). It also includes *doing* what is God's will. Like Christ, we must be righteous in *behaviour* as well as in being.

3⁸. The man who practises sin is not a child of God (see comment on 3¹), but of the Devil (see 3¹⁰, Mt 13³⁸⁻⁹).

'*sinneth from the beginning*'. John seems to be referring to John 8⁴⁴. From long before primitive man committed the first human sin, and until this day, the Devil has been a sinner (see *Note 12*, p. 56). It was because of his wiles that man first became a sinner. In a real sense, we are all responsible for our acts of sin, but God will make all allowance for 'the tempter's power'.

'*that he might destroy*' (i.e. undo). These words support the 'classical theory' of the Atonement, with its stress on the *victory* of Christ (see *Note 17*, p. 82).

'the works of the Devil'; i.e. the sins which are committed by those who are under his tyranny.

3⁹. '*begotten of God*'. See *Note 15*, p. 77.

'*doeth no sin*', '*cannot sin*'. See *Note 6*, p. 36.

'*his seed abideth in him*'. This phrase has been variously translated. (*a*) Moffatt takes '*seed*' to mean 'children' (cf. Jn 8[33]) and '*him*' to refer to God. He translates, 'the offspring of God remain in Him'. But, if this is John's meaning, he could have expressed 3[9] much more simply. (*b*) A more probable translation is, 'a divine seed (i.e. principle of life: *RSV*, 'nature') abideth in him (i.e. the man who is born of God)'. Dodd prefers such a translation and, comparing 3[9] with 2[24] and James 1[18], 1 Peter 1[23], Luke 8[11], thinks that the '*seed*' is the preached word, the gospel, which is thought of as regenerating the nature of the Christian, so that he does not sin (*CHD*, pp. 77-8). But, if we turn to John 1[13], 3[5, 10] and to the comments on 2[20, 27], we see that it is the *Holy Spirit* who imparts the divine principle of new and spiritual life into the believer, so that he is born of God. Perhaps we should paraphrase: 'A principle of new life, imparted by God through the Holy Spirit, abides in the man who is born of God.'

3[10]. '*In this*' refers to what follows. Regenerate men are '*children of God*' (see comment on 3[1]), unregenerate men are still '*children of the devil*' (see 3[8], Jn 8[41, 44]). And now, says John, I will give you a practical test whereby these two groups can plainly be distinguished.

'*loveth not his brother*'. The man who does not practise '*righteousness*' is not a child of God. But 'righteousness' is too vague a definition of Christian morality. John now narrows it down to that supreme and basic virtue which the heretics are so signally failing to practise—love of the brethren (see *Note 11*, p. 52). So 3[10] leads on to the next test, that of 3[11-24a].

NOTE 17. THE VICTORY OF CHRIST*

There is no orthodox theory of the Atonement. If all the metaphors which have been used to explain it were piled on top of each other, the whole mass could not adequately express the mystery of the Cross. But every one of these metaphors—a revelation of God's love, an exposure of man's sin, an expiation, a satisfaction, a sacrifice, and even such words as 'propitiation' and 'substitution' if properly safeguarded—shows some different aspect of the saving work of the Crucified. None of these aspects should be absent from our preaching. It is not enough to tell our people that 'Jesus saves'. We must be able to answer the questions which leap into their minds, even while we preach the Cross; questions which usually begin with

* A summary of what I wrote in *The Raven*, No. 7.

an awkward 'Why?' or 'How?', and which, if unanswered, may block the sinner's path to the feet of his Saviour. Gustav Aulén of Sweden, in *Christus Victor*, has revived our interest in the 'classic' or 'dramatic' conception of the Cross which dominated the thought of the early Church; a conception which is certainly prominent in the mind of John. It may briefly be summarized.

(*a*) *Christ's whole life was a deliberate offensive against all the powers of evil.* He came '*that he might destroy the works of the devil*' (3⁸). Therefore He began His ministry by engaging the enemy of man in deadly combat in the wilderness (Lk 4¹⁻¹³), and through His life He continued that offensive. Every 'mighty work' was a binding and despoiling of the Strong One (Mk 3²⁷). When the Seventy gave their mission report, He saw 'Satan fallen as lightning from heaven' (Lk 10⁸).

(*b*) *The offensive of His life came to climax in the offensive of the Cross.* Towards the end, He 'steadfastly set his face to go to Jerusalem' (Lk 9⁵¹). He approached the Cross with serene and deliberate self-direction (Jn 10¹⁸). He was not dragged to it; He strode to it. To the end He waged uncompromising warfare against the demonic enemies of man. A few days before Calvary, He foretold the Devil's defeat and His own triumph (Jn 12³¹⁻²). Even when Satan seduced Judas (Jn 13²), He could still claim that 'the prince of the world' had no power over Him (Jn 14³⁰). And so, an hour or so before His arrest by the Devil's agents, and almost in sight of the Cross, He boldly proclaimed His victory before it had been won. He said, 'I have overcome the world' (Jn 16³³). Only the last agony remained, and then the glory (Jn 17⁴⁻⁵). His handful of followers deserted Him and He went on alone, to challenge the enemies of God and man to crown or crucify Him. He went on, to win or lose a world's salvation. It was as critical as that.

(*c*) *The offensive of the Cross issued in the victory of the Cross.* Against that solitary figure, seemingly so defenceless, there were flung in those last hours all the unseen powers of evil. The Devil used every weapon on his armoury (pride, prejudice . . . complete the list) and, of course, he used human agents—he always does. At the end of that black day, his arsenal was empty; and what happened? If Jesus had used his power to come down from the Cross, if he had hated those who condemned Him to the Cross and those who hung Him on it, evil would have won the day, and God would have been defeated. But Jesus prayed for His murderers (Lk 23²⁴) and loved them, as He loved all men, to the end. Because He prayed thus, He died in triumph. His last cry was one of exultant victory; 'It is finished' (Jn 19³⁰)! The Devil had done his worst, and in so doing he had received what would prove to be his death-blow. By crucifying the Son of God, the Saviour of men, he had sealed his own final doom. Christ's work was consummated, Satan's tyranny was for ever broken, God's triumph was won, and mankind was redeemed.

(*d*) *The victory of the Cross was proclaimed on Easter Day.* It was not *won* on that day; it was won on Good Friday. But if the gospel story had ended, 'And they crucified Him', the victory of the Cross would have been won, but nobody on earth would have known it. The Christian Faith would not have survived and the Church would never have been born. The exultant hymns of Easter *announce* the victory that has already been won.

(*e*) *Mopping-up operations.* This talk of Christ's victory and the Devil's defeat sounds strange to us today, for we are very conscious of the presence and power of the Devil in our own lives and in the life of the modern world. Here a now-familiar illustration will help us. The battles of Stalingrad and El Alamein really settled the issue of the second World War; the war was 'as good as over' though the fighting dragged on for years and with costly casualties. Just so, the victory of Christ on the Cross settled the issue with the Devil and his dark angels, and with the sin that is reigning in men's souls and in the world's life; but the fighting goes on, and will go on for centuries. The Devil is doomed, but refuses to admit it, and will do as much damage as he can before his final end. But the warfare which continues in the Christian and in the world is really in the nature of 'mopping-up operations'. God's *final* triumph may be long delayed, but it is inevitable.

How can Christ's victory become *our* victory? That question is dealt with in *Note 25*, p. 114.

(*b*) 3¹¹⁻²⁴ᵃ. The Test of Genuine Loving

3¹¹⁻¹⁸. Summary: *He who obeys Christ's command of love is a child of God and already has eternal life. He who hates his brother is a child of the Devil and on his way to death. We must love to the uttermost, but we must also express our love in humble deeds of sacrificial giving.*

3¹¹. Once Christ is accepted as Saviour, He must be obeyed as Lord. His offer of eternal life is immediately followed by tremendous demands, and the supreme ethical demand is that of love of the brethren in the fellowship of the Church, and love of all mankind (see comment on 2⁷, and *Note 11*, p. 52).

3¹². What a terrible illustration of the ultimate result of dis-obedience to the divine command of love, and what a contrast to the Christian's love of his fellow man—whether he is a good or a bad man—is that Devil-inspired hatred which caused Cain to murder Abel because he could not tolerate his brother's goodness.

3¹³ runs on from verse 12, and does *not* start a fresh paragraph. Christians must not be surprised if, for the same reason, they are hated by '*the world*' (see *Note 7*, p. 38), just as the perfect Jesus was hated. This hatred is the inevitable counter-attack of wickedness against goodness, of paganism against Christianity. As in 3⁷⁻¹⁰, so in 3¹¹⁻¹⁵, John seems to be thinking of John 8³⁷⁻⁴⁷, which should be studied.

3¹⁴ᵃ. '*We know that*'. On Christian Certainty, see *Note 27*, p. 124.
   '*out of death into life*'. This reminds us of John 5²⁴, where Jesus tells the Jews that those who accept Him and obey Him have 'passed out of death into life'. We Christians, says John, have passed out of 'the world', which is the realm of lovelessness and therefore of death, into the family of God, which is the realm of love and therefore of real life. We know, says John, that we belong to God's family and possess eternal life, because we can meet the test of genuine loving; '*we love the brethren*' (see *Note 11*, p. 52). Some of them are far from saintly; they are touchy and quarrelsome, or ambitious for office, or intolerant of our point of view, or prejudiced against us; but we do not despise their immaturity or resent their attitude to us. Others are far saintlier than we are, but we are not irritated by their spiritual superiority; rather we are stimulated by the challenge of it. We love them all; but—and this is the point—not in our own strength. Born into God's family, we have received from Him a supernatural life and a supernatural power to love all men.

3¹⁴ᵇ⁻¹⁵. The same truth, in negative form. John re-states the teaching of Jesus that hatred is as deadly and blameworthy as murder, for it is incipient murder, whether or not it issues in the fatal deed (Mt 5²¹⁻²). It is obvious, therefore, that the man who seeks to destroy life in others cannot possess the principle of eternal life within himself.

3¹⁶. '*Hereby know we love*'; not 'the love of God' (*AV*). John says that the word "*agapē*" has been given an entirely new content by the fact of the Incarnation and its consummation in the supreme sacrifice of the Cross; here is revealed the very essence of true '*love*' (see *Note 9*, p. 45). In *The Acts of John*, a Gnostic

G

interpretation of Christianity published about A.D. 160, Christ is represented as a divine Being quite incapable of suffering and death. While the spectacle of the Cross—a pure illusion—is being watched by the mob, Christ is pictured as calmly talking to His disciples on the Mount of Olives. (See Docetism in *Note 14*, p. 68.) What a fantastic distortion of the truth! Whatever else the Cross means, it is an astounding revelation of the costly, redemptive love of God for men (cf. Rom 5⁸, Gal 2²⁰).

'*and we ought*'. In 2⁶, John has called us to imitate Christ; he now says that this imitation must go to the very limit of self-giving (see Jn 13³⁴). We ought to be willing to surrender life itself for love of one another. In every age, some—few or many—have been called upon literally to make this costly sacrifice. The whole army of martyrs is not confined to early Christendom, nor does the Church's Roll of Honour contain only such names as those of Protestants who died for the Reformation faith, or of heroic missionaries who never returned from what we used to call 'the foreign field'. But whether or not we are called upon to *die* for love of others, the principle is unaffected; our love must be an utter love which recognizes no limits and refuses no sacrifice (cf. Rom 16⁴). Christianity is no life for arm-chair adventurers, but for girt soldiers, stout-hearted crusaders, who are ready to take their life in their hands and willing to give it for others, as and when Christ requires. The Gates of Hell cannot prevail against such valiant lovers of God and their fellows, for you cannot defeat a man who is already bearing his cross and following Christ.

3¹⁷. '*goods*'. The Greek word means 'physical life', but here it stands for the means of maintaining that life; its material necessities; what Jesus called 'our daily bread'.

'*shutteth up his compassion from him*'; slams the door of his heart against him. By contrast, see Mark 1⁴¹, 6³⁴, etc.

In this verse, John moves from the plural to the singular; from '*brethren*' to '*brother*'. It is easier to be enthusiastic about Humanity with a capital 'H' than it is to love individual men and women, especially those who are uninteresting, exasperating, depraved, or otherwise unattractive. Loving everybody in general may be an excuse for loving nobody in particular. It is when the general becomes the particular that we find it so difficult to 'love' the man next door whose dog habitually ruins our bedding-out plants, the ladies in the railway-carriage who chatter all the way to the terminus, or the acquaintance who rings up on the telephone when we are listening to the final instalment of a television serial. The cynic who said, 'I love humanity, but I don't like people', reminds us of the doctor in Dostoevsky's *The Brothers Karamazov*, who says to Father Zossima, 'I have often made enthusiastic schemes for the service of humanity, and perhaps I might even have faced crucifixion for humanity, if it had been suddenly necessary. And yet I cannot live in the same room with anyone for two days.' The love for others which Jesus requires of us is not an omnibus emotion, but a personal relationship with people, one by one.

But John also moves from the sublime to the mediocre, that he may stress the practical nature of genuine love, and its day-to-day relevance. We shall probably never be called upon to die for our brethren. John therefore warns us against that sentimental heroism which cries, 'I am ready to die for my fellows', but which is not interested in the everyday needs of men and women. We are to have a sincere and steady concern for the individual at every point of his need, whether that need be great or small, spectacular or commonplace; and our 'charity' must go beyond the provision of mere material help (see Mt 25^{31-46}). The taciturn milkman whose only conversation is a growl, the derelict old charlady who steals out of your office as you stride into it, those Jamaican immigrants who are lodging in your road and 'have rather let down the tone of the neighbourhood'—have you made any effort to discover their needs and tried to meet them? Are other people's needs quite as much your concern as your own necessities? If not, you don't love them; and how, then, can the '*love of God*' (i.e. your love for God) be the master principle of your living? See *Note 11*, p. 52.

3^{18}. To protest that we love people, but to fail to put our love into action; to express deep sympathy with those who suffer from poverty and disease, from the calamity of earthquake and plague, from the tyrannies of communism or apartheid and from ravages of war, but to make no effort to relieve their sufferings, is just insincere tongue-wagging. It costs us nothing. And this, by the way, is one of the things that make preaching the most perilous of occupations; the utterance of pious sentiments as a substitute for costly action. Let us remember Matthew 7²¹, James 1²², 2¹⁵⁻¹⁷. Love must not only be felt and voiced; it must be expressed in '*deed*' and reality.

3¹⁹⁻²⁴ᵃ. Summary: *By living this life of love, we may be sure that we are the children of God. With a clear conscience, we can offer our petitions to our Father, for we are doing His will. And this is His will, that we should believe on His Son and obey His command of love. Doing so, we live in union with God.*

3¹⁹⁻²⁰. '*Hereby*', as used by John, normally refers to what *follows* (as in 2³, ⁵⁻⁶, 3²⁴); but here (as in 4⁶) it refers to the *previous* verses. By living this life of genuine love, we '*know that we are of the truth*', i.e. that we belong to God's family and share His nature.

'*assure*'. The usual meaning of the Greek word is 'persuade', and we can translate, 'shall persuade our heart *that* we are of the truth', the 'that' clause being supplied from the first half of the verse. But the verb can also mean '*assure*' (*RV*), 'reassure' (*RVS*), 'still' (Brooke). This, probably, is what John means. We can reassure our heart, we can still our conscience.

We must now choose between two possible renderings of verses 19b-20, ignoring less likely versions (see *CHD*, pp. 88-92, *AEB*, pp. 98-101). (*a*) The *AV* treats these verses as a *warning* against complacency, since the '*we know*' may lead to over-confidence. The sin which still lurks in our hearts may escape *our* scrutiny, but it cannot escape God's. But, to bring out this meaning, we have to supply such words as are printed in brackets in this paraphrase: 'By living this life of genuine love, we know that we belong to God and we reassure our conscience in His presence. [But we must be absolutely confident that our love is genuine] for if our [own] conscience condemns us [in this matter, let us remember that] God is greater than our conscience, and knows all things [and His judgement will be much more searching].' But could John expect his readers to supply these bracketed words? Besides this, John has already given warning after warning against insincerity and self-deception, but in this passage his purpose is to *encourage* believers in a settled confidence that they belong to God. (*b*) Therefore, we must accept the *RV* translation, and paraphrase as follows: 'By living this life of genuine love, we know that we belong to God and we reassure our conscience in His presence, whenever our conscience condemns us; because God is greater than our conscience, and knows all things.' John is warning his readers—and us—against an over-sensitive conscience. In our highest moods, we *know* that our love for others is genuine, and that it is the result of our sharing of God's nature, to whom we belong. But in our lowest moods, accusing thoughts remind us of our failures to carry love into action, and the old feelings of guilt and fear return to destroy our confidence. But, says John, the fact that God knows all things must comfort, not dismay you; for He knows that, despite occasional failures (which He will forgive), you *are* His devoted children, and your love of others is genuine (cf. Jn 21¹⁷). This encouraging message is needed by Christians who suffer from a morbid sense of guilt; who spend too much time in taking themselves to pieces, fingering their motives, measuring their spiritual blood-pressure, and poking about among their guilty memories, until sin becomes an unhealthy obsession.

3²¹. If we allow God to deal with our over-sensitive conscience, so that it no longer torments us, and to encourage us to reassure ourselves in His presence, then we can always approach Him with that humble confidence which John calls '*boldness*', and which includes freedom of speech (see comments on 2²⁸, 4¹⁷).

3²². Another result of this practice of genuine love for others is that our prayers are offered with confidence, and become effective. God will answer them because '*we keep his commandments*' (see comments on 2³⁻⁴), which can be summarized in the word 'love', and Christian love is always '*pleasing in his sight*'. In one way or another, our heavenly Father will always answer the petitions of those who are one with Christ in spirit and the deeds of love (see Jn 15⁷; cf. 14¹⁴⁻¹⁵, 16²⁶⁻⁷). But the contrary is also true. When we fail in love for our fellows, and treat them with loveless indifference, resentment or jealousy, the conscious or unconscious effect of our failure is to hinder our approach to Father. Our prayers lose their wings; our thoughts stumble and we know our petitions are ineffective.

3²³. '*commandment*'. See comment on 2³.

'*believe in the name*'. Belief is mentioned for the first time. On its meaning, see *Note 18*, below.

'*love one another*'. See *Note 11*, p. 52.

The whole will of God is summarized in this verse as Christian belief issuing in Christian behaviour; whole-hearted faith in Christ as God's Son and man's Saviour, and a resultant and unreserved love for '*one another*'—that is, for all mankind. Paul sums it up as 'faith working through love' (Gal 5⁶). This intimate connection between belief and behaviour, between faith and works, is dealt with in *Note 19*, p. 92.

3²⁴ᵃ. '*his commandments*' looks back to verse 22. In this verse, 'his', 'him' and 'he' refer to God, though what John says is equally true of Christ.

'*abideth in him* [God], *and he* [God] *in him* [the obedient believer]'. For the first time, John refers to the *mutual* indwelling; not only 'we in God', but also 'God in us' (see *Note 10*, p. 48). This divine side of our fellowship is stressed in the next chapter.

Verses 23-24a form a transition to the next section; from the test of *genuine loving* to that of *true believing*.

NOTE 18. 'BELIEVING' AND 'BELIEVING IN'

The noun '*pistis*' (= 'faith') never appears in John's Gospel, and only once in his Epistles, in 5⁴ (see). He prefers the corresponding verb, '*to believe*', and W. F. Howard suggested a reason for this preference. By A.D. 100, there was a tendency in some Churches to regard 'faith' as a fixed system of doctrinal truth. It almost came to mean 'orthodoxy', as in James 2¹, Jude 3, 20. John used the verb rather than the noun to stress the fact that faith is not mere assent to a set of theological propositions, like the Apostles' Creed, but that essentially it is a dynamic, personal relationship with the living Christ.

Faith in Christ, indeed, must *begin* with a certain minimum of intellectual conviction, and to express this element in faith John uses the verb '*to believe*' in the sense of 'to give credence to', 'to assent to a communicated truth', So, in 3²³, '*we should believe (in) the name of his Son Jesus Christ*' means 'we should give assent to the truth that Jesus Christ really is what His name implies Him to be—the Son of God and our Saviour'. In 5¹⁰ John says, '*he that believeth not God*'; i.e. 'he who does not accept as true what God has said in history, and especially in the life and ministry of His

Son' (cf. Jn 4²¹, 5²⁴, ³⁸, 8⁴⁵⁻⁶, etc.). In the same sense, John uses '*to believe that*'. In **5¹**, '*believeth that Jesus is the Christ*' refers to an intellectual assent to a statement about Jesus, as does the similar phrase in **5⁵** (cf. Jn 6⁶⁹, 11²⁷, 13¹⁹, etc.).

But, when John refers to full, saving faith, he uses '*to believe on*', and by this he means a man's self-commitment to God in Christ in utter trust and devotion. In John's Gospel, Christ calls on men to '*believe on*' Him in this sense, that they may gain eternal life (Jn 3¹⁶, ³⁶, 6³⁵⁻⁴⁰, 11²⁵⁻⁶) and John divides people into those who 'believe on' Him and those who do not (e.g. Jn 2¹¹, 4³⁹, 7⁵, 8³⁰, 10⁴², 12³⁷). So, in **5¹⁰**, John comes to this conception of full, saving faith. '*He that believeth on the Son of God*' means 'he who assents to the truth that Christ is the Son of God, *and* commits himself to Him in utter trust and devotion'. So also, in **5¹³**, '*you that believe on the name of the Son of God*' means all that **3²³** (above) means, *plus* 'and commit yourselves to Him in utter trust and devotion'.

This contrast between '*believe*' (give assent) and '*believe on*' (commit yourself) is seen in John 6²⁹⁻³⁰, 8³⁰⁻¹, and it is also seen in the '*believeth on*' and '*believeth*' in **5¹⁰**.

Faith in Christ, therefore, must begin with a certain minimum of intellectual acceptance. This does not mean, as some critics suggest, that Christianity consists in 'the docile and unintelligent acceptance of a mass of antiquated dogmas'. It does mean that saving faith must be *grounded* on certain basic convictions—that God is our heavenly Father, that Christ His Son came to earth to be our Saviour, and that, by His life, death, resurrection and continuing presence, He has made possible our salvation. We preachers must labour to bring our hearers to this initial conviction by proclaiming the central truths of the gospel. But intellectual assent to the truth that Christ is the divine Saviour of mankind must develop into an unreserved commitment to Christ as *my* Saviour, 'who loved *me*, and gave himself for *me*', in a response of confident reliance—what John Wesley quaintly called 'a recumbency upon Him'—and complete devotion. Our answer to the question, 'What must I do to be saved?' (Acts 16³¹) is that of Paul to the Philippian jailor, '*Believe on* the Lord Jesus'. It was of such faith that Charles Wesley sang:

> *By faith we know Thee strong to save;*
> *Save us, a present Saviour Thou!*
> *Whate'er we hope, by faith we have,*
> *Future and past subsisting now. (MHB 362)*

Then, when intellectual assent has become personal commitment, we must help our people to think out the implications of their faith, that they may fortify themselves against doubt, communicate their faith to others, and defend 'the faith' against sceptics and heretics.

NOTE 19. BELIEF AND BEHAVIOUR

In 3²³, summarizing the 'commandment' of God, John intimately joins together Christian belief and Christian behaviour. He does not say 'belief *resulting* in behaviour', but the whole message of his letter shows that that is what he means. Constantly Jesus taught that faith in Him must issue in Christian conduct; e.g. Matthew 7¹⁵⁻²³, where He says that 'By their fruits ye shall know them', and that those who call Him 'Lord', but fail to live out that belief in deeds, are not true believers. This necessary union of 'faith' and 'works' is prominent in Paul's epistles. In *Romans*, for instance, his thesis on Saving Faith (Chapter 1-11) is followed by a Manual of Christian Conduct, the two sections being significantly linked together by the word 'Therefore' (Rom 12¹). John does not divide his letter into (a) Theological, (b) Ethical. Throughout the letter he shows that our attitude to Christ and our attitude to our fellows is an inseparable unity, just as Jesus did in the discourse of John 13-16. Do we really '*believe on*' Jesus Christ, and thereby '*know*' the Father and are in intimate union with Him, so that already we possess 'eternal life'? Always, says John, the test is, 'Are we living out this faith in everyday behaviour, in unfailing obedience to the supreme command of our Lord that we "*love one another*"?' See also 5¹.

John Wesley insisted that genuine faith in Christ will always be ethically creative, and must be lived out in the life of 'perfect love'. Of his 44 Standard Sermons, 20 of them deal with our faith, and 24 of them with the ethics of the Christian life. At the 1766 Conference in Leeds, it is significant that Wesley, speaking about personal religion, asked these practical questions about the Methodists: 'What servants, journeymen, labourers, carpenters, bricklayers, do as they would be done by? Which of them does as much work as he can? Set him down for a knave that does not. Who does as he would be done by in buying and selling, especially in selling horses? Write him knave that does not. And the Methodist knave is the worst of all knaves.'

The fact that Christian behaviour is inseparably linked with a vital Christian faith is tragically illustrated, in reverse, in the life of modern England, and especially in the serious deterioration in our standards of personal morality. Basil de Selincourt once said, 'England still remains a Christian country in the sense that we cleave together in a profound realization that the kind of life called Christian is more worth living than any other'—but is that true today? Those ideals of personal and social life which once seemed second nature to us, and those homely virtues which used to characterize the life of our average citizen, all sprang from the Christian faith; but how long can a Christian code of life survive, when Christian faith has vanished? Neitzsche was a true prophet when he said: 'Now that the belief [in the Christian God] has been undermined, all that was built on it and was one with it must collapse; for instance, our entire European morality.' Somehow we Christians must convince our contemporaries of the sheer folly of imagining that men can enjoy all the privileges of a Christian civilization, without holding any real Christian belief. By living lives of startling and supernatural love, we must witness to the supernatural faith which inspires such living—and surely men will find it hard to resist such a self-authenticating witness to the saviour-hood of Christ.

> *What we have felt and seen*
> *With confidence we tell,*
> *And publish to the sons of men*
> *The signs infallible. (MHB 377)*

and the 'signs infallible' are the deeds of Christian love which are the result of our 'believing on' Jesus Christ.

(c) 3²⁴ᵇ-4⁶. The Test of True Believing

Summary: *We know God remains within us, from the witness of His Spirit. The heretics claim to be inspired by the Spirit, but they cannot meet the test of true believing, as you can. They are inspired by the spirit of the Antichrist and are really children of the world; that is why the world listens to their propaganda, and not to ours.*

3²⁴ᵇ. *'we know that'*. See *Note 27*, p. 124.

In verses 23-24a, John has returned to the thought of union with God in Christ (see *Note 10*, p. 48); he now says that our guarantee of this divine indwelling is *'the Spirit'* whom God (or Christ) has given us, and whose presence assures us that we are really at-one with God in Christ (cf. Rom 8¹⁵⁻¹⁷, and see *Note 20*, p. 96 on the Johannine doctrine of the Holy Spirit). This is the first specific mention of the Spirit in *1 John*, and we expect John to develop the theme, but for the time being his mind is sidetracked. He returns to the witness of the Spirit in 4¹³, but again fails to enlarge on it; indeed he does not do so until 5⁷.

4¹. Mention of the Spirit reminds John that *one* of the gifts of the Spirit is inspiration, and that the heretics who have just resigned their membership and *'gone out into the world'* (see 2¹⁹) had been regarded as inspired *'prophets'* in the Asian Church. In the first century, the apostles were the supreme doctrinal authority, for they could bear witness to the actual facts of the gospel. Subordinate to them were the '*prophets*' (1 Cor 12²⁸, 14¹⁻⁵, Eph 4¹¹); men who, under the influence of the Holy Spirit (Jn 16¹³) interpreted these facts and declared their significance in each developing situation. But, as Paul discovered, this prophetic liberty must always be disciplined by the basic facts of the gospel, and John knows that this discipline is urgently needed in his own day. It seems that the heretics claimed that their superior knowledge of God had been imparted to them by His Spirit—probably in ecstatic experiences, and that this special revelation made the primitive faith out-of-date and inadequate. But, says John, '*believe not every spirit*'. (On 'believe' as 'give credence to', see *Note 18*, p. 90.) Rather, '*prove*' (= test) them (cf. 1 Thess 5¹⁹⁻²¹). Prophets may be inspired, not by the Holy Spirit, but by evil spirits; they are therefore '*false prophets*' (see Deut 13¹⁻⁵, Jer 14¹⁴, Mk 13²²).

In 3²³, John has summed up Christianity as *belief* and *behaviour*. He now shows that the heretics are false prophets because they cannot meet either test; the test of *belief* (4²⁻⁶), or that of *behaviour* (4⁷⁻²¹).

4². Paul had written that the man who cries out 'Jesus is accursed' cannot be inspired by the Holy Spirit, but only he who can say 'Jesus is Lord' (1 Cor 12³); but, since his day, heresy had taken a more subtle and dangerous form. The Asian heretics could confess Christ as 'Lord', and yet deny the doctrine of the Incarnation. John, therefore, gives a more exact definition of belief in the person of Christ as a test of orthodoxy; a test which his readers can apply for themselves. See *Note 14*, p. 68.

4³. John says that this subtle form of heresy, which claims to be a higher form of Christianity, and yet rejects its foundation truth, is inspired by an evil spirit; that '*spirit of the antichrist*' to which he has already referred in 2¹⁸⁻²³, and which is now threatening the faith of the Church (see *Note 13*, p. 67). We must bring the same charge against the modern heresy of a 'reduced' Christianity. The man who reveres Christ as the noblest of all men, but denies that He was in any sense divine; the man who accepts the 'divinity' of Christ, but only in the sense that He was uniquely God-inspired, and not God-incarnate; the pietist who accepts the 'spiritual' gospel of Christ, but ignores its moral and social implications; the social reformer who accepts the ethical and social teaching of Jesus, but ignores the fact of human sin and the redeeming power of a divine Saviour—all these are *'false prophets'*, inspired by the spirit of Antichrist, and not by the Spirit of Christ.

4⁴. John's readers belong to God, and God is more powerful than *'he that is in the world'*, the Devil, the 'prince of this world' (see *Note 12*, p. 56). Because God's Spirit dwells in them, they have not only *'overcome'* the Evil One, resisting his temptings (2¹³⁻¹⁴), but they have also *'overcome'* the heretics, by rejecting their specious arguments and their false claims to be divinely inspired. On *'overcome'*, see also *Note 25*, p. 114.

4⁵. The heretics, failing to win the Church to their 'new theology', have left it and begun their own missionary work in pagan society—and, for the time at least, their propaganda tours have met with a success which is alarming some of the faithful. John seeks to reassure them. As he has said, these people have never really been members of the Church (2¹⁹); their true home is *'the world'* (see *Note 7*, p. 38), and the innovations they have tried to introduce into Christianity are derived from pagan wisdom. It is no wonder that they are serious rivals, for pagans are more likely to welcome this compromise between Christianity and Gnosticism than the true faith (cf. Jn 15¹⁹).

4⁶. *'We'* here means 'We orthodox teachers who speak for the whole Church'.

'he that knoweth God' (i.e. he who belongs to God and is coming to have a vital experience of Him) will listen to our message—just as *'he who is not of God'* will ignore it (cf. 1 Cor 2¹¹⁻¹²). This statement, like such words of Jesus as Matthew 11²⁵, John 8⁴⁷, 10²⁷, suggests that some people are potential Christians by their very nature, and others are not. And does not Paul seem to believe in predestination (Rom 8²⁹⁻³⁰)? Are there two sorts of people; those who by nature have an affinity with God, and those who are completely worldly? Does this explain why some people listen to our preaching, and others will have none of it? This is a mystery—and John is not really dealing with it; his only purpose is to encourage the faithful

by assuring them that the success of the heretics must be a limited success, for those who really belong to God will not be led astray (see *CHD*, pp. 100-2). But, if asked to debate this difficult question, John would probably point to what he has written in 2^2 and 4^{14} ('for the whole world'; 'Saviour of the world') and tell us that we must still hope and pray that, in His own way, God will yet win to Himself those who seem to be incorrigibly indifferent, or even hostile, to Him. Indeed, can we forget how, again and again in every age, men and women who seemed to be out-and-out worldlings have been soundly converted to Christ and transformed into devout believers?

'*By this*', contrary to John's normal usage, refers *back*, to verses 2-6a. One test as to whether a man is inspired by the Holy Spirit, the '*Spirit of truth*' (see Jn 16^{13}), or by the Antichrist, '*the spirit of error*', is whether he accepts or rejects the confession of verse 2, and does or does not '*believe in the name of his Son Jesus Christ*' (3^{23}).

NOTE 20. THE HOLY SPIRIT AND THE INDWELLING CHRIST

Apart from a concealed reference in 2^{20}, the Holy Spirit is mentioned in *1 John* only in 3^{24b}, 4^{13}, 5^{7-8}, and in none of these passages does John develop anything like a doctrine of the Spirit. Indeed, we may regret that, at 3^{24b}, he was drawn into a digression on true and false inspiration (see comments on 3^{24b} and 4^1). But I think we may take it for granted that, whenever he mentions the Spirit, he has in mind Christ's teaching about the Paraclete which he has recorded in John 14-16. This seems to be confirmed by 5^7, where '*the Spirit of truth*' has an obvious reference to John 14^{17}, 16^{13}. In 2^1, Christ is the Paraclete, but in John 14-16 Jesus speaks of 'another Paraclete', and this 'Other' is so closely associated with Himself that He seems to think of Him as His *alter ego*—His own self in a different form. So, in John $14^{16, 26}$, the Father will *send* the Paraclete; in 16^7, Jesus Himself will *send* Him; but in $14^{18, 20, 28}$, it is Christ Himself who will *come* to them. In 14^{17}, He says that the Spirit 'shall be in you'; in 15^4, He says, 'I in you'. In 14^{17}, 16^{13}, He speaks of 'the Spirit of truth'; in 14^6, He says, 'I am the truth'. Almost identical, and yet 'another'!

It is significant that, when Paul is thinking theologically, he can distinguish between Christ and the Holy Spirit (*KG*, p. 53), but in his *experience* he cannot do so. In Romans 8^{9-11}, he does not distinguish between 'the Spirit of God', 'the Spirit of Christ', and 'Christ'. In 1 Corinthians 3^{16}, Galatians 5^{24-5}, we are indwelt by the Spirit; in 2 Corinthians 13[5], Galatians 2[20], by Christ. Luke has the same difficulty. In Acts 16[6-7], the route of Paul and his companions is directed by 'the Holy Ghost' and 'the Spirit of Jesus'; see also 1 Pet 1[11-12]. In many of our great hymns, we find the same significant confusion between the work of Christ and that of the Holy Spirit in the life of the Christian.

When we try to define the difference between the Indwelling Christ and the Holy Spirit, we may say that God gives Himself to us, objectively, in the person of His incarnate Son, but that He actually *imparts* Himself to us in the person of the Holy Spirit. We may say that Christ comes into the life of the Christian and of the Church *through* the Holy Spirit. But, as a matter of *experience*, we shall be true to the mind of Jesus and the New Testament writers if we think of the Spirit as 'the Spirit of Christ'; Christ Himself, freed for ever from the limitations of His human life, and living within the Christian and within the Church in the person of His 'Other Self', thus fulfilling the promise of Matthew 28[20]; 'Lo, I am with you alway'.

So, when John says that God abides in the Christian (3[24], 4[12-16]), and adds that we *know* this because God has given us the gift of the Spirit (3[24], 4[13]), he means that we know that God permanently dwells in us because, as a matter of joyous experience, we are absolutely convinced that, in the person of His *alter ego*, Christ is active within us, ever empowering, inspiring, guiding and enlightening us, and assuring us that we have really been born of God and are now members of His family (cf. Rom 8[15-16], and see comment on 5[7]).

(C) 4[7]-5[13]. THE TESTS OF LOVE AND BELIEF.

(B) 4[7-11]. The Test of Genuine Loving (resumed)

Summary. *When we love, we show that we have been born of God and that we know Him, for God is love. He showed His love for us when He sent His own Son to give us eternal life and save us from sin. Then surely we, who are so loved by God, must love one another.*

In 3[23], John summed up the 'commandment' of God as (a) Belief, and (b) Love. In 3[24b]-4[6], he dealt with (a), using it as his third test of belonging to God's family. Now he turns to (b), and so *resumes* his second test of 'Genuine Loving', continuing the thought of 3[11-24a].

4[7]. Appealing to his readers to '*love one another*', John bases his appeal on the fact that '*love is of God*'; i.e. that love belongs to the very nature of God, and so our love for others has its origin in Him (see *Note 9*, p. 45, and *Note 11*, p. 52). It follows that the man who loves has experienced the new birth and been '*begotten of God*' (see *Note 15*, p. 77), for he is sharing God's nature. It also follows that he '*knoweth God*' (see *Note 8*, p. 43).

4⁸. If he does not love, he has not begun to know God, for '*God is love*' (see *Note 21*, p. 99, on **4⁸, ¹⁶**).

4⁹. This verse is a restatement of John 3¹⁶, which Luther called 'the gospel within the gospel', and which is never far from John's mind.

'*sent*'. In John's Gospel, Jesus uses the phrase 'he who sent me' no fewer than 26 times, and this must have been in John's mind when he used the word '*sent*', here and in verses 10 and 14. Luther once said: 'If I were as our Lord God, and these vile people were as disobedient as they now be, I would knock the world in pieces.' But God did not abandon His 'human experiment'; nor did He impassively wait in high heaven for sinful men to grope their way up to His footstool, pleading for pardon and a second chance. The word 'sent', like 'gave' in John 3¹⁶, stresses the astounding fact that God so loved us that He took the initiative and '*sent*' His own Son on a redemptive mission which could only be fulfilled at awful cost to both the Father and the Son. How almost incredible is the passion of that divine love which, knowing the sacrifice, the shame, the outrage, the agony which must be endured, '*sent*' His Beloved to live and die for our redemption. We feel something of the wonder and the cost of it when we study this verse, or John 3¹⁶, Romans 8³². Surely the conception of a God who cannot suffer is a theological illusion. 'God is not glorified by crediting Him with an infinite stoicism' (*GGF*, p. 336).

'*only begotten Son*' (cf. Jn 1¹⁴, ¹⁸, 3¹⁶, ¹⁸). Christ was uniquely *the* Son of the Father. Therefore He, and He only, reproduced the nature and character of God in their fullness, so that His revelation of the Father to men is unique and complete. On God's love for us, see *Note 16*, p. 79. On '*live*', see *Note 2*, p. 17.

4¹⁰. On our love for God, see *Note 9*, p. 45.
'*propitiation*'; see comment on **2²**.

4¹¹. On the motive of our love for '*one another*', see *Note 11*, p. 52.

NOTE 21. GOD IS LOVE

The meaning of '*agapē*' has been studied in *Note 9*, p. 45, and God's love for a world of sinners in *Note 16*, p. 79; but John's statement that '*God is love*' (4⁸, ¹⁶) calls for further study. Here John says something about God which men could never have argued themselves into believing. The idea that the one, supreme God could, and actually does, love such people as ourselves—as an idea—is quite unthinkable; besides it would suggest that God is not complete and self-sufficient in Himself. The amazing truth that '*God is love*' is a revealed truth; it has been revealed in action in all God's dealings with the human race, but supremely and finally in the person and life of His incarnate Son (see *Note 16*, p. 79). We see Jesus loving depraved tax-collectors and abandoned harlots, as well as decent men like John and Peter; the brutal soldiers who scourged Him and nailed Him to the Cross, as well as the gentle women who ministered to Him in Bethany: we see Him dying that He may save, not only those who are devoted to Him, but those who engineered His crucifixion—and we cry, 'This is God in action'—and only then can we accept the incredible truth that '*God is love*'; universal, unchangeable love. That is why, when we sing,

> '*Tis love! 'tis Love! Thou diedst for me!*
> *I hear Thy whisper in my heart:*
> *The morning breaks, the shadows flee,*
> *Pure, universal Love Thou art;*
> *To me, to all, Thy mercies move:*
> *Thy nature and Thy name is Love* (*MHB* 339, 340)

we are not only saying something about Jesus; we are describing the nature of God Himself. That is why we sing, of Jesus, '*Emptied Himself of all but love*', for if He had emptied Himself of love, He would have ceased to be divine.

We now see *why* the love of God is spontaneous and uncaused (see *Note 16*, p. 79); *why* He does not love us because we are worthy of His love; *why* He loves the atheist as well as the believer, the Communist as well as the Christian, the intolerant Sectarian as well as the ecumenically minded Churchman, the pervert and the gangster as well as the pure and devout. He loves us, unlovely as we are, because it is His *nature* to love; because He must love. '*He hath loved, He hath loved us, because He would love*' (*MHB* 66).

But what of the fact of evil and suffering in a world which is governed by this God of love? The rationalist who pictures man as a lonely and battered individual, struggling against the whole weight of a heartless universe which cares nothing for his hopes and fears, joys and tragedies, rejects the fundamental Christian revelation that, at the heart of the universe and all human experience, is the God whose character is unchangeable and undefeatable good-will. The Christian must hold on to that basic fact, though he may find it impossible to explain hospitals for incurables, earthquake disasters, or such hells on earth as Belsen and Buchenwald.

The 'attributes' of God are governed by love, the essential nature of God; His holiness is the holiness of love, His omnipotence is the omnipotence of love, and so on. We must never think, for instance, of God's justice as conflicting with His love, of His wrath as something different from His grace. This is the mistake Bertrand Russell makes when he criticizes the character of Jesus because He denounced the hypocrisy of the worst type of Pharisee. He fails to see that our Lord's denunciation was the expression of His loving purpose to expose all sin that He might save every sinner. The 'Gentle Jesus, meek and mild' of our childhood prayers is also the Jesus whose eyes 'are as a flame of fire' (Rev 1^{14}). Love cannot compromise with evil; it must oppose it with its own holy passion until it is destroyed. God's wrath is not the absence of love; it is the outworking of it. Everything He does is the expression of His fundamental nature, which is *love*.

4$^{12-16}$. **Summary:** *That brings me back to the thought of our union with God. No mortal can see God; but if we love one another we have union with Him. Let me put it another way. We cannot see God, but we have seen Christ, the incarnate Son, our Saviour, and through believing on Him we have union with God, and know how He loves us. 'God is love', I have said, and to live in love is to live in God.*

In 2^5 and 3^{24}, John has partly answered the question, 'How do we *know* that God abides in us and we in Him?' He now completes his answer.

4^{12}. '*beheld God*'. In the Old Testament, Moses and others are said to have 'seen' God (Gen 15^1, 20^3, Ex 33^{11}, Num 12$^{6-8}$, Deut 34^{10}, Isa 6$^{1-5}$, Ezek 1^{28}), but in various ways the fact is stressed that these 'visions' must not be taken too literally (see Ex 33$^{20, 23}$). In Matthew 5^8, Jesus says that the pure in heart shall 'see God', but this promise refers to the life hereafter. Paul probably refers to seeing God in 1 Cor 13^{12}, but says, 'now we see in a mirror darkly', in contrast to the face-to-face vision of the future. In this world, God is the 'invisible God' (Col 1^{15}, 1 Tim 1^{17}). In the Prologue to his

Gospel, John plainly says, 'No man hath seen God at any time' (Jn 1[18]; cf. 5[37]), which is repeated almost exactly in this verse (4[12]; cf. 4[20]). In 3[2], he has said that *we shall see* God, but in the hereafter. Through the ages, mystics have aspired to face-to-face 'vision of God', and perhaps the heretics, like many of their Gnostic contemporaries, were claiming to have this mystic vision of God, whereby unique knowledge of God was given them. John has no word of encouragement for them. But there is a sense in which the Christian can 'see' God, even in this life. Jesus said to Philip, 'He that hath seen me hath seen the Father' (Jn 14[9]; cf. 1[14], 12[45]). As we live in the gospel story, we 'see' the glory of the character of God expressed in the person and ministry of His Son (cf. 1[1-3]).

God is invisible, but His *presence* within us is proved by the fact that *we love one another*'; see *Note 11*, p. 52. In 4[7], John says that this love shows that we are 'begotten of God'. Here he says that it shows that '*God abideth in us*'.

'*his love*'. Scholars differ as to whether this means God's love for man, or man's love for God; it could mean either. But the last phrase in this verse is so similar to '*hath the love of [for] God been perfected*' in 2[5], that '*his love*' surely means 'his love for God' (see *Note 9*, p. 45).

'*is perfected*'. On Perfect Love, see *Note 22*, p. 102.

4[13]. In 3[24b], the indwelling Spirit of Christ witnesses to the Christian that God abides in him; here the same witness confirms the *mutual* indwelling; '*we abide in him, and he in us*' (see *Note 10*, p. 48).

4[14]. The witness of the Spirit in 4[13] reminds John of another witness; the eye-witness of those who '*beheld*' the incarnate life of the Son of God (see comment on 1[1]). On '*sent*', see comment on 4[9]. On '*Saviour*', see *Note 23*, p. 104. On '*the world*', see *Note 7*, p. 38.

4[15-16]. John returns to the *conditions* of the mutual 'abiding' of the Christian and God. In 3[24], he says that the condition is obedience to the commandment of God, which (in 3[23]) he sums up as (*a*) belief in Christ and (*b*) love for one another. In 4[15], he says again that one condition is (*a*) belief in Christ. In 4[16] (cf. 4[12]), he says again that the other condition is (*b*) love for God, including love for one another.

4¹⁵. '*confess that*'; see comments on **2²³**, **4²**. John's readers will understand that '*confess that*' means not only '*believe that* Jesus is the Son of God', but also '*believe on* Him and unreservedly commit himself to his divine Saviour' (see *Note 18*, p. 90).

4¹⁶. '*we*', as in **4¹⁴**, means John and his fellow-eyewitnesses, but of course it also includes all who have come to have a real experience of Christ as Saviour. On the meaning of **4¹⁶ᵃ**, and on the relationship between '*know*' and '*believe*' in John's thought, see *Note 24*, p. 106.

'*God is love*'; see comment on **4⁸**, and *Note 21*, p. 99.

'*abideth in love*'; see comment on **4¹⁵⁻¹⁶**, above. Since God is love, he who unfailingly lives a life of love to God and his fellow man is sharing the very nature of God Himself, and so lives in intimate union with Him and has that 'experience' of Him which John calls 'knowing God'. On the other hand, the man who claims to '*know*' God, but does not love Him, may be some sort of a theologian; he is no sort of a Christian.

NOTE 22. PERFECT LOVE

John Wesley said the doctrine of 'Christian Perfection' is best described as the doctrine of 'Perfect Love', and he took this phrase from *1 John*. John says that our love for God is '*perfected*' in so far as we obey His commands (**2⁵**), including the command to love one another (**4¹²**), and that if we live this life of '*perfect love*' we shall be bold and without fear when we come to our day of judgement (**4¹⁷⁻¹⁸**). The doctrine of perfection was prominent in the writings of the Apostolic Fathers, but in subsequent ages it was often neglected. In the eighteenth century, it was John Wesley and the Methodists who reinstated it as one of the central doctrines of Christianity, though it gave great offence to many. The man who said to a Methodist preacher, 'The doctrine of perfection is not calculated for the meridian of Edinburgh' was typical of many objectors. Indeed, the doctrine is not prominent in modern preaching—even in some Methodist preaching; sometimes because of a natural reaction against the extravagant claims of some Holiness sects; more often, perhaps, because of a misunderstanding as to the true meaning of the doctrine.

At conversion, the *process* of sanctification begins, but as we have seen (see *Note 6*, p. 36) there is no New Testament support for the idea that entire sanctification immediately follows the new birth. John admits that the believer is still a sinner and liable to occasional acts of sin. But we have also seen that the believer is *expected to be sinless*. Can that expectation be realized in this life? Certainly Jesus said, 'Ye therefore shall be perfect, as your heavenly Father is perfect' (Mt 5⁴⁸), and He told the young ruler what to do if he would be perfect (Mt 19²¹). He endorsed the commandment that we should love God with *all* our being (Mk 12³⁰) and prayed that His disciples might be perfected (Jn 17²³). Paul used such phrases as 'unblameable in holiness', 'perfecting holiness', 'perfect in Christ', 'the perfecting of the saints', and urged his converts to press on towards the goal of perfection (1 Thess 3¹³, 2 Cor 7¹, Col 1²⁸, Eph 4¹², Phil 3¹²⁻¹⁶). John is just as emphatic when he says, 'Whosoever is begotten of God doeth not sin . . . and he cannot sin' (3⁹; cf. 3⁶, 5¹⁸). Paul and John agree that the converted man need no longer be defeated by the power of sin, for Christ has broken its tyranny. The Christian should live in a mood of confidence in present victory over evil's domination, believing that, in any crisis or temptation and by the power of the indwelling Spirit, he can perfectly love God and manifest this love in action. And certainly we must accept, in principle, the possibility of perfect love in this life as a divine-human achievement, for how can we fix a limit to the power of the indwelling Christ? Surely He can not only save *all*, but to the *uttermost*?

But can we call it a 'practical ideal', as Wesley did? Is it not like saying to a schoolboy who is struggling with the nine-times table, 'Now let us do some quadratic equations'? Of course it is, if we are thinking of that *absolute* perfection which, under the conditions of this life, we shall never achieve. That is why Wesley never spoke of 'sinless perfection'. At every stage in our progress towards entire sanctification, our love for God can only be *relatively* perfect. (*a*) Our knowledge of God and of His will is a growing knowledge, and therefore our conscience is ever in need of re-education and we are constantly in danger of committing *sins of ignorance*. At any moment we may be humbly confident that we really do love God 'perfectly' and yet, before long, we shall make some new discovery of God's nature and will, which will challenge us to press forward to a *more* perfect love and more perfect expressions of it in conduct. (*b*) Our knowledge of ourselves is also a growing knowledge. In our pilgrimage to holiness, we may come, as Wesley said we could, to a stage when we never consciously and deliberately rebel against God and commit high-handed sin; but sin, that perversion of a man's *whole* being (see *Note 5*, p. 35), affects his *unconscious* as well as his conscious being. Again and again, we discover unsuspected tendencies to sin which have been lurking within us. For instance, many a devout Christian is discovering, today, that his attitude to black and coloured people has been one of unconscious arrogance. Only gradually, as the cleansing power of the Spirit operates in the hidden depths of our being, is mastery given us over this 'inbred sin'. In the *Collect for Christmas Day* ('Grant that we being regenerate . . . may daily be renewed by Thy Holy Spirit'), our *daily* need of re-conversion is recognized. For these two reasons, the more saintly a man becomes, the more sensitive he is to the sin that remains in him, and to the fact that other sin has yet to be discovered.

Someone has said that the major problem of the preacher is the man who says, 'Lord, save me; but not yet, and not altogether'. Too many of us are cases of arrested development. Dr Rainy of Edinburgh once said to his students: 'Do you believe that a day is coming, really coming, when you will stand before the throne of God, and the angels will whisper together, How like Christ he is?' That is how we must challenge ourselves and our hearers. We must never encourage the heresy that Christ requires '*perfect love*' from only a select minority of saints. The Medieval Church made a fatal error in teaching that 'seculars' could be saved from 'mortal' sins, but that only members of religious orders could obey the 'counsels of perfection'. Jesus recognized no double standard of devoutness, no pass and honours degrees in holiness. He meets us in the rush and turmoil of everyday life, amid the tensions and problems of modern society, and says, 'Ye shall be perfect'; and every one of us must pray: 'Cleanse the thoughts of our hearts by the inspiration of Thy Holy Spirit, that we may *perfectly* love Thee.'

NOTE 23. JESUS CHRIST, SAVIOUR

The word '*Saviour*' means one who delivers others from threatening disaster; but what sort of disaster? In the Old Testament, the prevalent idea of salvation was deliverance from national enemies, and those who led Israel to victory in critical days were known as 'saviours' (Judges 3[9], 2 Kings 13[5], Neh 9[27]). Since it was God who inspired and directed such 'saviours', He Himself was *the* Saviour of Israel (Ps 106[21], Isa 43[3], 45[15, 21], etc.). The average man of today also thinks of 'salvation' in terms of deliverance from external evils (war, political tyranny, racial and class prejudice, economic insecurity, etc.), or evils which threaten his physical or mental wellbeing (poverty, disease, fear, anxiety, etc.). Having no effective faith in God, for the last half century and under the direction of popular Humanists he has been trying to work out his own 'salvation'. He has been fooled into thinking that man is inherently *good* and will do the good when he *knows* it, and so has believed that, by means of universal education, the programme of this or that political party, and the discoveries and inventions of modern science, he can be his own saviour. What he has yet to discover is that, even if he could effect this 'salvation'—and he has almost abandoned hope of doing so—he would still be far from solving his real problem; that what is wrong with his life (and therefore with world-life) is something which is wrong within himself, not physically and mentally, but spiritually.

When Jesus was born, the Jews had come to see that salvation is essentially salvation from *sin*, and they thought of the expected Messiah as their coming Saviour, in that, when He had inaugurated God's reign on earth with a great Judgement Day, He would vindicate all righteous Jews as the true people of God. But to deserve this verdict the individual Jew must *become* righteous, and (the Pharisees said) this they could only do by strictly obeying every command of the divine Law. But this was really a call to self-salvation, and few Pharisees discovered, as Saul of Tarsus did, that a sinner *cannot* save himself from sin; see Romans 7^{14-24}, which seems to be a diary which Paul *might* have written during the months before his conversion, describing his growing despair of ever working out his own salvation. There are still many well-meaning people who are trying to get rid of sin by constant effort and good resolutions, with occasional prayers to God in emergency. They cannot do it. By nothing he can ever do will the sinner be able to get rid of the guilt of the past; by no effort of his perverted and weakened will can he change himself from a sinner into a saint. John Wesley tried to do so for twelve long slogging years, and failed. So shall we. Man cannot save himself; he can only *be* saved by a divine Saviour.

Only once in the New Testament is it explicitly stated that Jesus came to save us from *sin* (Mt 1^{21}), but this is clearly taken for granted (see *Concordance* under 'save'; eg. Mk 10^{26}, Lk 19^{10}, Jn 3^{17}, 12^{47}, Eph 2^8, 1 Tim 1^{15}). Even more startling, in the earlier New Testament writings Jesus is rarely called 'Saviour' (only in Lk 2^{11}, Acts 5^{31}, 13^{23}, Eph 5^{21}, Phil 3^{20}). To Jewish Christians, 'Christ' came to mean much of what we mean by 'Saviour'. By the end of the century, however, when Gentiles outnumbered Jews in the Church, and when, moreover, the emperor was blasphemously worshipped as 'God' and 'Saviour', the phrase 'Jesus Christ our Saviour' sounds like a trumpet call through the later New Testament writings; once in *2 Timothy*, three times in *Titus*, and five times in *2 Peter*. But nowhere is the saviourhood of Christ more strongly stated than when John writes, '*The Father hath sent the Son to be the Saviour of the world*' (4^{14}; cf. Jn 4^{42}); Saviour from *sin*, and not (as the Gnostics held) Saviour from *ignorance*. But in what sense, in *1 John*, is Christ our Saviour from sin?

(1) *He saves us by revealing the essential character of God.* In His human life, but supremely in His death (3^{16}), He revealed God as a God of love, and disclosed His saving purpose for mankind. Thereby He imparts to believers that knowledge and personal experience of God, and that intimate union with Him, which give 'eternal life' or salvation.

(2) *He saves us by revealing the awful nature of sin.* He declared God's loving purpose to make us into His children (3¹). But, through sin, we have fallen under the tyranny of evil and become the children of the Devil; the sort of people who hung Christ on the Cross and murdered Him (3⁸⁻¹²). It is when we see the enormity of sin, that we turn from it with loathing and turn towards Christ who came to save us from our sin (3⁵).

(3) *He saves us by delivering us from the guilt of sin.* He is the 'propitiation' for our sins, the means by which we are forgiven (see comment on 2²). He is also our 'Advocate' with the Father (see comment on 2¹). So, if we have done with self-deceit and confess our sins, God is 'faithful and righteous to forgive us our sins' (see comment on 1⁸⁻⁹).

(4) *He saves us by delivering us from the power of sin*, and John stresses this in two ways. (*a*) Through union with Him and a new birth, Christ abides within us and, in so far as we surrender ourselves to His divine power, He 'cleanseth us from all sin' (see comment on 1⁷ᵇ) and makes it possible for us to live the life of 'perfect love'. (*b*) Christ came to destroy the tyranny of the Devil (3⁸) and has won an everlasting victory over him. True believers can share this triumph and 'overcome' the Evil One and the attacks of his agents (2¹³, 5⁴).

If Christ is our Saviour *from* sin *into* eternal life, He can also save us from spiritual death (3¹⁴), from unnerving fear (4¹⁸), from frustration and defeatism (2¹³, 5⁴), from the sense of the futility of life (2²⁵), and from all other deadly enemies.

NOTE 24. KNOWING AND BELIEVING

What John means by '*knowing*' God (see *Note 8*, p. 43) and '*believing on*' God (see *Note 18*, p. 90) are not contrasted as an either-or, but are closely related. Indeed they stand side by side in 4¹⁶ᵃ; '*We know and have believed the love which God hath in us*'. But what is the relationship between 'know' and 'believe' in this verse? Since '*we*' particularly refers, as in 4¹⁴, to those who have been eye-witnesses of Christ's ministry, it may help us if we briefly outline the reaction between the 'knowing' and 'believing' of the first disciples, as it is recorded in John's Gospel. Their first *knowledge* (= mere acquaintance) of Jesus soon gave rise to a *belief* (= credence) that He was the expected Christ (Jn 1⁴¹, ⁴⁵), and this in turn issued in a more intimate knowledge (= experience) of Jesus. Soon this gave rise to their first expression of trust and self-committal; 'his disciples *believed on* him' (Jn 2¹¹). But Jesus was a strange Messiah, very different from their expectation, and so, during the next two years, knowledge and belief, experience and trust, reacted on each other in the minds of the disciples, until we come to John's record of what took place at Caesarea Philippi. Peter says, 'We have *believed* [that] and have come to *know that* you are the Holy One of God' (Jn 6⁶⁹, *RSV*; cf. Mk 8²⁹). By this time, a growing experience of Jesus had resulted in a more intelligent *'believe that'* (credence), and this had been established in a firmer *'know that'* (confidence). But in the previous verse Peter shows that they are not only sure that He is the Christ; they have committed themselves to Him in trust and loyalty (='*believe on*'). But their spiritual pilgrimage is not over. As yet they do not even grasp the truth that Jesus will one day be crucified; much less that He in whom their trust is not a holy Man sent from God, but is actually God-incarnate. So, even in the Upper Room, Jesus is not satisfied when they say, 'Now *know* we *that*' and 'by this we *believe that*' (Jn 16³⁰). He calls them to a fuller self-committal (Jn 14¹) which shall finally bring them to that full confidence in and experience of Himself (Jn 14²⁰) which is the very essence of eternal life (Jn 17³).

Now return to 4¹⁶ᵃ—and here I owe much to the generous guidance of C. K. Barrett. In view of the whole context, and John's distinctive use of the verbs '*know*' and '*believe*' with '*God*' or '*Christ*' as object, it seems that what John really means by this compressed sentence is something like this: 'We have come to *know* Christ, who has revealed the love God has for us, and indeed we have come to *believe on* God, whose love has been so revealed.' Through their confession of and self-committal to Christ (4¹⁵), John and his readers have come to '*know*' (to have an established and intimate experience of) Christ and His revelation of the love of God (cf. 2³⁻⁴, 4⁷, 2 Tim 1¹²). As a result, they have come to '*believe on*' God in an even more complete self-committal, and so the process will continue, faith and knowledge acting and reacting on each other throughout their spiritual pilgrimage.

We can trace this same process in our own experience. Mere acquaintance with the facts of the Gospel story; then belief that these facts are true; then an experience of Christ as a pleading and challenging presence; then a 'dive into the deep end' in an act of 'believing on' or self-surrender to Him; then a confident knowledge (experience) of Christ as Saviour; then a fuller self-committal; and so on, from fuller faith to deeper experience to fuller faith . . . continually. What we must never do is to settle down at any stage of this process, and be satisfied with the extent of our faith and the depth of our experience of God and His love.

4¹⁷⁻²¹. Summary: *Through this union, our love for God is perfected, so that we may be confident when we come to our judgement-day. Perfect Love cancels all fear. Our very capacity to love is our response to God's love for us; but our love must be for our*

> *fellows as well as for God. The man who says*
> *'I love God', and does not love his fellows, is living*
> *a lie. Besides this, God has commanded us to*
> *love both Him and man.*

4¹⁷. '*Herein*'. Scholars differ as to whether this phrase refers forward to the rest of the verse, or back to the last clause in **4¹⁶**. Probably the latter. By this double indwelling, our love for God is perfected (see *Note 22*, p. 102).

'*with us*' probably means no more than 'in us'. It may mean 'on our part'; so *AV*, 'our love'.

'*boldness*'. See comments on **2²⁸** and **3²¹**.

'*the day of judgement*'. One of the results of our perfected love will be that we shall '*have boldness in the day of judgement*'. This reminds us of **2²⁸**; and what John means by '*the day of judgement*' must depend on what he means by '*at his coming*' in that verse. But what did Jesus teach about judgement?

Jesus accepted the Jewish belief that human history would end in some sort of universal judgement, but there is not much evidence that He thought of a mass gathering of all humanity at the throne of God and a universal '*day of judgement*'. His *unique* teaching was that the divine judgement is already and continuously in operation (Jn 3¹⁸⁻²¹, 5²⁴, 12³¹, 16¹¹). He did not come to be Judge, but Saviour (Jn 3¹⁷, 12⁴⁷), and men are inevitably and immediately judged by their response to Jesus Himself and His revelation of the Father. If they commit themselves to Him, they stand approved; if they reject Him, they stand condemned (Jn 3¹⁸⁻²¹, 12⁴⁷⁻⁸). By this same principle of present judgement, 'the world' itself stands condemned (Jn 12³¹; cf. Lk 11³⁰⁻²). If divine judgement is present and continuous, it follows that the final judgement at the end of history will not be an investigation into our deserts; it will be a final manifestation or 'finalizing' of divine judgements which *have already been made* on each individual man and on each nation or civilization.

If, in **2¹⁸, ²⁸**, John was thinking of the end of history and the final *parousia*, here he must be thinking of the final Day of Judgement of popular belief. But every age in which evil comes to threatening climax, and is revealed in all its demonic power, is in a sense a '*day of judgement*'. Were not John's readers living in such an age (see comments on **2¹⁸, ²⁸**), and was not what he said about the Christian's '*boldness*' relevant to their situation, even though their '*day of judgement*' did not turn out to be the final Judgement Day? And are we not living in such an age today; an age in which a decision is demanded—faith or unbelief, for or against Christ? Only if our response is one of utter self-committal to Christ, so that He abides in us and we in Him, can we have a quiet conscience in this judgement-time and boldly witness to our generation of the only Saviour of the world (see comment on next verse).

For the individual man, *every* day—and especially every day of special emergency and trial—is a day of judgement, for divine judgement is present and continuous. Only in so far as we live the life of constant devotion to God, through His unhindered indwelling, can we daily endure the searching glance of Christ, and remember His presence with '*boldness*' and peace of heart. But there is yet another, a final day of judgement, for all of us, when our earthly course is run and we step into eternity. If, and only if, the very mainspring of our life has become a constant love for God, we shall face the inevitability of death with a confident mind, and when we sing about it we shall not need to transpose the music into a minor key. Whenever we meet our Lord, today, tomorrow, the other side of death, we shall not shrink from Him in shame, but be bold to approach Him and humbly adore Him.

> *No condemnation now I dread;*
> *Jesus, and all in Him, is mine!*
> *Alive in Him, my living Head,*
> *And clothed in righteousness divine,*
> *Bold I approach the eternal throne,*
> *And claim the crown, through Christ, my own.*
> (*MHB* 371)

'*because, as he is*'. The word translated 'he' (literally 'that one') generally stands for the exalted Christ in *1 John*. Perfect love gives us this boldness '*because*', in so far as we are living this life of love, we are conforming to the pattern of Christ's own character and life (see comments on 2⁶, 3³, ¹⁶). He is our Judge, but we are '*as he is*'.

4¹⁸. On '*perfect love*', see *Note 22*, p. 102.

'*casteth out fear*'. In the Old Testament, 'the fear of the Lord' is prominent, but this represents an elementary stage in religious experience. It is true that Jesus told His disciples to fear only God, since He alone held their destiny in His hands (Lk 12⁴⁻⁵), but they were then in the kindergarten of disciple- ship. As John says, this fear of God *'hath punishment'*; that is, 'has to do with punishment' (*RSV*). At the earliest stage in his spiritual life, the sinner is halted in his career of sin by the realization that he is rebelling against an almighty and holy God, and that if he continues to do so, he must take the consequences. This is a necessary discipline for the sinner, but the mature Christian has outlived this fear of God, for *'perfect love'*—the response of unreserved love to the infinite love of God—*'casteth out fear'*. John does not say, Love God, for fear of what He will do to you if you do not. Rather, he says, Love God to the utmost of your capacity for love, and you will never again shrink from Him in fear, for *'there is no fear in love'*. Fear is essentially self-centred. It asks, 'What is going to happen to me?' and dreads the answer. But when our love for God is perfect—even though only 'relatively' perfect—self is forgotten and only devotion and adoration remain. All we are now justified in fearing is any undiscovered, and therefore unsanctified, impulse which might lead to action which would add another wound to the Christ of the Cross, and grieve the heart of our Father.

But in a wider sense than this, *'perfect love'* for God *'casteth out fear'*. It should make the Christian fearless of both hostile men and adverse circumstances. He will no longer dread death and what may happen after death, but more than that; when life in its grimmest moods threatens all that he holds most dear, he will face it unafraid. What changed the far from rock-like Peter into the fearless leader of the persecuted Christian community was the fact that he could say to the risen Christ, 'Lord . . ., thou knowest that I love thee' (Jn 21¹⁷). As the body of John Knox, the great Scottish Reformer, was being lowered into the grave, someone said: 'Here lies one who feared God so much that he never feared the face of man.' A finer epitaph would have been, 'Here lies one who *loved* God so much . . .'. Modern man needs this message, for fear is the dominant disease in this 'Age of Anxiety'; an age in which thousands of people are neurotics, mental hospitals are over- crowded, and the suicide rate is alarmingly high. It is not enough to urge the man who is in the grip of fear to use his utmost will to master it; the human will has its breaking-point.

Rather we must convince him that only those who have a vital faith in Christ, who live in Him and thereby live a life of constant love and devotion to God, can face days of crisis with stout confidence, and fearlessly adventure themselves into the unknown future.

4¹⁹. On this important verse, see *Note 9*, p. 45. John resumes the thought of **4¹⁰,** and reminds us that our very capacity for love is not the result of our own will-power; it is imparted to us, inspired in us, by God who loves us infinitely, and in so loving us has shown us the meaning and the wonder of love and has created it within us.

4²⁰. '*I love God*'. A man may say this, but what he means by '*love*' may be a warm emotion, and nothing more. This is not what Christ or the Christian mean by love (see *Note 9*, p. 45).

'*hateth his brother*'. There is nothing between white and black, love and hate, in John's vocabulary; no in-between greys. He is thinking of a professing Christian who is indifferent to the needs of his fellow Christians, and may even positively dislike—or hate,—a member of the Church to which he belongs. He says that a man who piously says '*I love God*', but who fails to love one of his 'brethren', is a plain '*liar*'. If, as John has just said (**4¹⁹**), our very capacity for love is our grateful and self-giving response to the undeserved and amazing love of God for us (see *Note 9*, p. 45); if, as a result of our love for God, we live in such intimate union with Him that we share His very nature, so that love becomes 'second nature' to us; if this is true, it follows that a man who says 'I do not love this particular brother and I do not see that his needs are any concern of mine', shows that love is *not* his 'second nature', and therefore that he does not really love God.

'*his brother whom he hath seen*'. The meaning of the tense is 'whom he has continually before his eyes' (Plummer). John says: 'Every day of your life, you come face to face with brethren who are in need of your active love. What opportunities for putting love into practice! If you refuse to take them—if the only activity of your love is to glow with devotion towards the invisible God—you prove that your so-called love for God is bogus, a mere pretence. You are living a lie'.

'*cannot*' here means 'proves that he does not'.

4²¹. Besides, says John, as I have already reminded you (**2⁷⁻¹¹, 3¹¹, ²³**), God commands those who love Him to love their fellows also. You cannot love God and at the same time disobey His express command. On this verse, see *Note 11*, p. 52.

> **5¹⁻⁵. Summary:** *See how closely related are belief and love.*
> *Through believing on Christ we become God's*
> *children, and it follows that we love all His other*
> *children. That is both natural and a matter of*
> *obedience to the Father's command. Does God ask*
> *too much of us? No, for He gives us power to live*
> *victoriously.*

5¹. Continuing the theme of **4⁷-5¹³** (see p. 97), John again shows how closely related are Christian belief and Christian love, and that jointly they test any man's claim to be in union with God.

'*believeth not*'. John again stresses the privileges of those who believe that Jesus is the Son of God (cf. **2²²⁻³, 3²³⁻⁴, 4¹⁵**). By this emphasis on '*believeth that*', John does not mean that salvation *merely* depends on acceptance of the orthodox doctrine of the person of Christ. It is true that he does not mention full saving faith (believing *on* Christ) until **5¹⁰**, but both his Gospel and his preaching must have made it unmistakably clear to his readers that the Christian is one who *believes that* Jesus is the Son of God, and who then *believes on* Him as his divine Saviour (see *Note 18*, p. 90).

'*Jesus is the Christ*'; see *Note 14*, p. 68.

'*begotten of God*'; see *Note 15*, p. 77.

'*whosoever loveth*'. Continuing **4¹⁹⁻²¹**, John now says that any lack of love for our brethren is strange and unnatural. In a human family, is it not natural for a man to love not only his father, but also his brothers and sisters, his father's other children? So, if we belong to God's spiritual family, it is surely *natural*—it ought to be inevitable—that we should love all the other members of that family.

5². This verse is ambiguous. Most scholars think that '*Hereby*' (as usually in *1 John*) refers forward to the following clause, and accept the *RV* translation But surely we know very well whether or not we are loving our fellow men, and are more likely to be uncertain as to whether we really love God. John certainly seems to take it for granted that we *know* whether or not we love our brethren in $3^{14-15,\ 17-19}$, 4^{20}. It seems therefore that C. H. Dodd is right in holding that in this verse '*Hereby*' refers back to 5^1. He translates, 'By this we know that, when we love God, we love the children of God' (*CHD*, p. 125). A fair paraphrase would be: 'I have said that it is *natural* that a child of God should love not only the Father, but all the Father's children. Therefore, when we love God and obey His commands, it follows that we inevitably love His children.' If we ignore, dislike or hate *any* man, we are not genuine Christians; but, John would say, if we adopt such an attitude to a fellow Christian, our behaviour is monstrously *unnatural* —as well as a matter of flagrant disobedience.

'*we love the children*'; see *Note 11*, p. 52.

'*love God*'; see *Note 9*, p. 45.

'*his commandments*'; see comments on 2^{7-8},

5^3. See 5^2. John now says that loving God and keeping His commandments are one and the same thing. He is surely thinking of what Jesus said in John $14^{15,\ 21,\ 23-4}$. Love for God is more than an emotion; it is also a constant state of mind and a set direction of the will. As C. L. Mitton says, it is 'a deep concern that God's will shall prevail' (*CLM*, p. 98). Obviously, therefore, our love for God can only be fully realized in absolute obedience to Him.

'*are not grievous*'; i.e. 'are not an intolerable burden'. Jesus did not disguise the fact that the loving God makes tremendous demands upon His children (e.g. see Mt $5^{20,\ 47-8}$, $6^{24,\ 33}$). But in striking contrast to the '*grievous*' burdens which the Pharisees imposed on their disciples—the hundreds of rules and regulations which they must obey because a strict God demands it (Mt 23^4)—the yoke of Jesus is easy and His burden is light (Mt 11^{30}). So, says John, the commandments of God are '*not grievous*'. Divine love demands that we offer a responsive love to Him and our fellows, but it creates within us the *power* to give this response (see next verse). Divine love commands, and human love, equal to the task, eagerly obeys; irksome duty becomes joyous achievement.

5^4 runs on from 5^3 and should read '*are not grievous, because . . .*'; because the Christian is empowered to obey these tremendous commands.

'*whatsoever*', rather than 'whosoever'. We might paraphrase, 'power is given to him who is born of God to enable him to overcome the world.'

On '*begotten of God*', see *Note 15*, p. 77.

'*overcometh the world*'. When John spoke of overcoming the world in 4⁴, he was thinking of the victory of the true Christians over the heretics who had left the Church and were now at work in pagan society. Now he turns back to 2¹³⁻¹⁷ and the thought of those pagan influences and pressures which oppose the Christian as he seeks to fulfil the exacting requirement of the divine love. On '*the world*', see *Note 7*, p. 38.

'*the victory . . . our faith*'. This is one of the many 'great texts' in *1 John*, and it is more fully studied in *Note 25*, p. 114.

'*our faith*'. As we have seen in *Note 18*, p. 90, it is only here that John uses the noun '*faith*'. It does not mean 'the faith', the orthodox system of doctrinal truth which we accept. The next verse makes it clear that it refers to the faith of the individual Christian who 'believes on' Christ as his Saviour.

5⁵. '*believeth that*'; see comment on 5¹.

NOTE 25. THE VICTORY OF THE CHRISTIAN

'This is the victorious power that overcomes (the evil powers which rule) the world—our faith' (5⁴ᵇ). When John gave this rousing battle-cry to the believing Church, he was surely thinking of Christ's words, 'Be of good cheer; I have overcome (the evil powers which rule) the world' (Jn 16³³), and of that victory over the Devil which Christ won on the Cross (see *Note 17*, p. 82, and *Note 23*, p. 104). In 5⁴⁻⁵, John answers the question, '*How* can the victory of Christ on the Cross give *present* victory to the Christian over those evil powers which are (*a*) resident within him, and (*b*) rampant in 'the world' outside, and which make it so difficult for him to obey God's exacting commands (5³)?

(*a*) In 2¹³⁻¹⁴, he assured his readers that they are already conquering these *inner* demonic powers; '*ye have overcome the evil one*'. In 2¹⁵, he defined these powers as the pagan ambitions and enticements of 'the world' which the Devil insinuates into their minds to lure them to destruction. But what is the secret of this overcoming? In 3⁶, ⁹, he gave one answer; the Christian '*cannot sin*' in so far as he is *born of God* and is really living in union with Him. In 5⁴ᵃ, he repeats this truth; it is the man who is *born of God* who overcomes the insidious temptations of '*the world*' to give God less than absolute devotion—and then he says the same thing in another form in 5⁴ᵇ. The secret of our victory is not any confidence in our 'better selves';

it is '*our faith*'. By our complete self-committal to and dependence on our Saviour, we share His life and energy and therefore share His victory over the Devil and all his invading demons. As we have seen in *Note 22*, p. 102, the converted man need no longer be defeated by those enticements of 'the world' which stimulate primal passions that are not yet sanctified, for Christ has broken their tyranny. Our personal life need no longer be a series of humiliating defeats at the hands of the Devil. Never again need we use the vocabulary of modern defeatism, and talk of 'impotence' and 'frustration'.

(*b*) But the '*victory*' of 5^4 had a wider scope. In 4^{3-4}, John reminded his readers of the demonic forces of pagan society, personified as the Antichrist, who were attacking both the Church and the individual Christian. 'In the world ye have tribulation' (Jn 16^{33}); how true that was! They were hated and persecuted by the Jews, Domitian would soon threaten the whole Church with extermination, and for the first time deadly heresy was endangering its faith. But, said John, '*greater is he that is in you than he that is in the world*' (4^4); and now he cries, 'This is the victorious power that overcomes the evil powers which rule the world—our faith' (5^4). With all the odds against them, let them never doubt that they are on the winning side; the consummation of God's victory over world evil is only a matter of time. Today, we are not so sceptical as we used to be about those 'principalities and powers' of which Paul wrote; those dark forces of evil and unreason which are at work in history and which express the Devil's will to thwart God and destroy mankind. We have seen them all too clearly at work in new pagan 'ologies and isms', skilled in the techniques of scientific barbarism, armed now with nuclear weapons of total destruction, and expressing themselves in every realm of world life. But, unlike our bewildered contemporaries, we do not face the future with grim stoical courage, or forget it in a mad whirl of pleasure, or trust in luck, or dope ourselves with the hope that progress must continue despite all set-backs; nor do we merge ourselves with the frustrated, the defeated, the depressed, and wallow in self-pity. Believing on Christ with utter confidence and without reserve, we partake of His indwelling power, and shall share in His coming victory over the onslaughts of evil in our own time (cf. Rom 8^{35-9}). Ours must be the attitude of Thomas Becket in T. S. Eliot's play, *Murder in the Cathedral*. When the priests bar the doors of Canterbury Cathedral against the assassins, the archbishop forbids them to do so and cries,

> *We have fought the beast*
> *And have conquered. . . .*
> *Now is the triumph of the Cross, now*
> *Open the door! I command it. Open the door!*

Christ had conquered the Devil and broken his power, and no evil could prevail against a man who had committed himself to Christ in utter trust.

> **5⁶⁻¹³. Summary:** *Our belief in Jesus Christ as the incarnate Son of God is based upon His Baptism and His Cross. Add to them the testimony of the Spirit, and we have a threefold, divine witness. This inner witness of the Spirit also assures us that God sent His Son to give us eternal life. It is that you may* know *this, that I have written this letter.*

In *RV* and *RSV*, verse 7 of *AV* is omitted. It is an editorial addition which first appeared in some obscure fifth-century Latin MSS (*CHD*, p. 293; *AEB*, p. 154-65). Verse 6 of *AV* is divided into verses 6-7 in *RV* and *RSV*.

5⁶. Several interpretations of this verse have been given; that it refers to John 19³⁴; that '*water and blood*' mean the sacraments of baptism and the eucharist; or that the words denote the cleansing and life-giving work of Christ. Such suggestions seem to miss the main point of John's argument. He has just said that the Christian wins his victory over the world by his faith in Jesus, the incarnate Son. Now he insists that the simple creed, 'Jesus is the Son of God', must be given its full value, as expressing the basic truths of the Incarnation and the Atonement. At the same time, he makes his final attack on those who claim to be Christians, but who deny these doctrines. As we have seen in *Note 14*, p. 68, Docetists like Cerinthus held that Jesus and Christ were two separate beings; that when the *man Jesus* was baptized in the Jordan, the *celestial Christ* descended upon him, and throughout his ministry used him as the medium of His divine revelations to men; that, when He had completed His revelations, Christ withdrew from the man Jesus and was not involved in the crucifixion; that he who died on Calvary was not the divine Victor of the Cross, but a broken and forsaken man.

To expound the true faith and to refute heresy, John says first that Jesus Christ '*came by water*'. Now the Docetists could, and perhaps did, say that Christ (as distinct from Jesus) '*came by water*' (i.e. when the man Jesus was baptized), but that is far from what John means. It was the fact that the human Jesus was none other than the incarnate Son that was declared by God at the baptism (Mk 1^{11}). In that hour, Christ dedicated Himself to the mission on which God had sent Him—to live a genuine human life, and in so doing to become man's Saviour. But, in the second place—and John says it most emphatically—Jesus Christ came also '*by blood*'. He flatly contradicts those who said that the Cross had nothing to do with our salvation. It had everything to do with it, he says. It was the climax and completion of His saving ministry, both as Revealer (**1^5, 4^9**), as Redeemer (**2^2**) and as Victor (see *Note 23*, p. 104). If Christ did not come '*by blood*', He may be our Teacher, our Enlightener, but He is not our Saviour (**4^{14}**).

5^7. The Spirit also '*beareth witness*' to the historical fact and the saving significance of the baptism and death of Christ (cf. Acts 5^{32}). Did not the Spirit empower Jesus for His ministry (Jn 1^{32}), and at the end of it did not Jesus promise to give the Spirit to believers as His *alter ego* (see *Note 20*, p. 96), to 'bear witness of him' (Jn 15^{26}), to interpret His whole life and teaching to them (Jn 14^{26}), and to guide them into 'all the truth' (Jn 16^{13})? They can rely on this inner witness, for '*the Spirit is the truth*' (see *Note 4*, p. 25, *Note 20*, p. 96, and comments on **2$^{20, \ 27}$, 4$^{2, \ 6}$**).

5^8. There is therefore a threefold witness to the fact and the saving significance of the incarnation, and '*the three agree in one*'; they unite in establishing the truth about the incarnate Son. How this witness affects believers is seen in verse 11.

5^9. As C. H. Dodd suggests, we shall better understand **5$^{9-10}$** if we first look at John 5$^{19-47}$, which John here seems to have in mind (*CHD*, pp. 131-3). Jesus has made tremendous claims about Himself, but this is self-testimony (verse 31), and it must be verified by other witnesses. He calls into the witness box (*a*) John the Baptist (verses 33-5), (*b*) His own saving works which are really the witness of God Himself (verse 36), and (*c*) the divinely inspired scriptures which point forward to Him (verse 39). Just so, in **5^9**, our faith in Christ as our divine Saviour is affirmed by a threefold testimony which is that of God Himself. When Jesus began His work at the Jordan ('*by water*') it was *God* who declared Him to be His Son, and commissioned Him to His saving ministry. When that ministry

I

ended in the perfect sacrifice and victory of the Cross ('*by blood*') it was *God* who publicly vindicated Him as the world's Saviour (and not a human martyr) by raising Him from the dead. And now it is *God* who, through the Spirit, gives us personal, intimate experience of our Saviour and interprets to us the meaning of His saving work. If we accept the evidence of a reliable *human* witness in everyday affairs, how confidently we ought to accept this *divine* evidence; it is the testimony which only God is competent to give, for it is about His own Son (see Mt 11²⁷).

5¹⁰. John now makes the important distinction between 'believe on' (or 'in') and 'believe'; see *Note 18*, p. 90.

To the man who confidently '*believeth on*' (trusts in) Christ, the saviourhood of Christ becomes a matter of personal experience, through the presence of His indwelling Spirit; '*he hath the witness in him*'. The Christ of the gospel story (from Baptism to Cross) is known as a living reality within his heart, where He carries on His transforming and life-giving ministry.

'*believeth not God*'. Here 'believe' = 'give credence'. The heretic who, like Cerinthus, believes only certain sections of the gospel story, and in particular rejects every event which witnesses to the fact that Jesus was the incarnate Son, is rejecting the testimony of *God* (see **5⁹**). He shakes his little fist in God's face and cries, 'I don't believe you'—and that makes God a liar (see **1¹⁰**). Modern man may think that he evades this dreadful charge by saying 'I don't reject the story of Jesus; I merely fail to see its relevance to me and the modern scene', but this does not clear him. John goes on to say, '*because he hath not believed in . . .*'; or, to bring out John's real meaning, 'because he has not put his whole trust in Him whom God has declared to be His incarnate Son'. The man who refuses to commit himself to Christ as his divine Saviour is really saying, 'I do *not* believe the gospel story that God came to earth in the person of His own Son to be my Saviour'. If he really did believe it, how could he fail to surrender himself to his divine Redeemer?

5¹¹⁻¹². This inner witness of the Spirit to the person of Jesus Christ also assures us that God sent His Son to give us '*eternal life*' (see *Note 2*, p. 17). If we live in union with Christ (see

Note 10, p. 48), this eternal life is ours, here and now. It is as simple as that. With Christ, we have real life; without Him, we are really dead (cf. Jn 3³⁶).

5¹³. Here, apart from an added postscript, John ends his letter. Thinking back from **5¹²** ('*hath the life*') through the letter to his opening paragraph ('*concerning the word of life*'), he says that his purpose in writing has been to make it possible for the true believer to *know* that he actually possesses '*eternal life*'. Compare this with the verse with which John originally meant to end his Gospel, John 20³¹. He wrote the Gospel that men might believe on Christ and so *possess* eternal life; he writes the Epistle that they may *know* that they possess it.

On '*know that*', see *Note 27*, p. 124.
On '*eternal life*', see *Note 2*, p. 17.
On '*believe on the name*', see *Note 18*, p. 40.

5¹⁴⁻²¹. POSTSCRIPT

5¹⁴⁻¹⁷. Summary: *This certainty makes us confident that, if our petitions are in harmony with His will, God will answer them. As for our intercession for a brother who has fallen into sin—unless it is deadly sin—God will answer that prayer too.*

5¹⁴. '*boldness*'. Twice John has used this word in reference to our judgement day (see comment on 2²⁸; also 4¹⁷). Now, for the second time, he speaks of '*boldness*' in prayer (see comment on 3²¹⁻²), using the word in its literal sense of 'complete freedom of speech'.

'*according to his will*'. God will not answer our prayers just because we, His children, ask Him to do so. There are definite conditions to be observed. Prayer is effective *if* it is in Christ's name (Jn 14¹⁴), *if* we who pray are in close union with Christ (Jn 15⁷), *if* we live the life of obedience to God (3²²), and *if* (John now says) our requests are therefore always '*according to his will*'. 'Prevailing prayers meet the purposes of God upon their march' (*GGF*, p. 401). Prayer is not a technique for using the power of God for the achievement of our private desires. It is the dedication of our will to God in which we invite Him to make us more serviceable for His purposes. A. E. Brooke quotes a Jewish saying: 'Do His Will as if it were thine, that He may do thy will as if it were His'.

'*hereeth us*'. God is deaf to selfish prayers. Only if what we ask for ourselves will enable us to do His work more effectively, will God *listen* to us.

5¹⁵. 'we have the petitions'. Jesus said, 'Whatever you pray for and ask, believe you have got it and you shall have it' (Mk 11²⁴, Moffatt). So John says that, if our prayers are such that God will *listen* to them, we know that we already *possess* what we asked for. Note the present tense. God *is* answering our prayer, though we may not know it at the time—and though, when we do realize that the answer has been given, it may be an answer we did not expect; perhaps so wonderful that we did not dare to expect it.

5¹⁶. John now turns from petition to intercession for others. He is not here thinking of that great host of men and women who must always claim an interest in our prayers because of their sufferings and sorrows, their struggles and frustrations, their heavy responsibilities, their missionary activities, and so on. He has reminded us that the Christian is still liable to commit occasional acts of sin (see *Note 6*, p. 36), and now he insists that Christians must not fail to intercede for any brother who has fallen into sin. He has rebuked those who are blind to the physical needs of their fellow Christians (3¹⁷); he would be just as critical of those who, smugly content with their privileges as the children of God, are indifferent to the spiritual needs of brethren who have failed in their struggle with fierce temptation and in their effort to subdue their passions to the will of God. He has called his readers to imitate Christ (see comment on 2⁶); he has also reminded them that Christ is 'our Advocate on high' (2²). It follows that they, like their Lord, must intercede for believers who have fallen into sin.

'*will give him life*'. We may offer such prayers to God with confidence, for we know that they are '*according to his will*' (see comment on 1⁹). In response to our intercession, '*God will give him life*'; i.e. God will renew in the sinning brother that eternal life which is only his so long as he lives in intimate union with God.

'*a sin unto death*'. John makes a striking distinction between sins which are deadly, and those that are not. On this difficult distinction, see *Note 26*, opposite.

5^{17}. '*all unrighteousness*'. When he says that some sins are not deadly sins, John is not minimizing the seriousness of *all* sin.

NOTE 26. A SIN UNTO DEATH

'*There is a sin unto death*'. A difficult phrase. John admits that the Christian may commit acts of sin (see *Note 6*, p. 36), but says that God will forgive him when he repents (1^9), and urges his readers to pray God to forgive him (5^{16a}). But when a Christian commits '*a sin unto death*', John does *not* urge them to intercede on his behalf. What kind or degree of sin is this that places the sinner beyond forgiveness because, presumably, he is incapable of repentance? It is generally agreed that John is thinking of the sin of *apostasy*, but on what grounds does he suggest that apostasy is unforgivable? In 5^7, he has said that the Holy Spirit bears witness, in the heart of the Christian, to the fact that Christ is his divine Saviour, and in 5^{10} that the believer who rejects this witness makes God '*a liar*'. This rejection seems to remind John of the words of Jesus in Mark 3^{29}: 'whosoever shall blaspheme against the Holy Spirit hath never forgiveness'. C. L. Mitton's interpretation of these words is helpful and convincing (see *CLM*, pp. 27-9). The critics of Jesus hate Him so much that they actually say that, in His works of healing, He is not inspired by God's Spirit, but by the Devil. It is this fixed antipathy which says that good is evil, this utter insensitivity to divine love in action before their very eyes, which Jesus calls blasphemy 'against the Holy Spirit', which 'hath never forgiveness'. But does Jesus really mean that His critics have become incapable of repentance? Surely C. L. Mitton is right when he suggests that Jesus is using the method of *over-statement* in order to emphasize a truth, just as He did in Mark 10^{25}, Luke 14^{26}. He is driving home the truth that sin against the Holy Spirit is the deadliest form of sin, and that, if persisted in, it can make repentance and forgiveness impossible.

In the same way, thinking in particular of those heretics who have left the Church, John says that the man who accepts Christ as his divine Saviour and begins to experience the transforming power of His Spirit in his heart, and then deliberately and defiantly turns apostate, commits '*a sin unto death*'. He rejects the inner witness to his Saviour; he even goes so far as to identify himself with Antichrist and denies the real divinity of his Saviour (4^3)—and this is the deadliest of all sins. If persisted in, it makes a man incapable of responding to Christ's appeal, incapable of forgiveness, and therefore incapable of eternal life. It issues in spiritual death, self-annihilation (cf. Heb 6$^{4-6}$). This is the truth that John drives home by an over-statement similar to that of Jesus, when he calls it '*a sin unto death*'. He reminds us of the deadly seriousness of sin, and of

its fatal consequences if we persist in it; we may even lose our
Saviour and forfeit our salvation.

But 'all things are possible with God' (Mark 10²⁷), and only God
can judge when a sinner has sinned past forgiveness. Surely we
Christians must go on praying for the worst of men, and especially
for 'backsliders'; and yet John seems to discourage us from doing so
—'*not concerning this do I say that he should make request*'. But
John had told his readers to pray with '*boldness*' (5¹⁴). Perhaps he
means that the sin of deliberate apostasy is so soul-destroying in its
consequences, that he cannot suggest that they should intercede
with such a *confidence* for apostates.

Most of us have had to try to help devout Christians who have
tortured themselves with the conviction that they have committed
the unpardonable sin, the '*sin unto death*', until it has driven them to
the verge of insanity. William Cowper, the poet, was only one of
many such tormented people. In my own experience, the first thing
to do has been to try to show them that, so long as they are *distressed*
at the thought of sins committed, they *cannot* have committed the
unforgivable sin (see *CLM*, p. 29.)

5¹⁸⁻²¹. Summary: *How wonderful are the certainties of the
Christian! I have already mentioned them, but
let me now summarize them. . . . And one last
word; be on guard against all substitutes for the
one real God.*

The note of strong certainty has sounded again and again
through the last four chapters, and it dominates this closing
paragraph; see *Note 27*, p. 124.

5¹⁸. Compare verse 18a with 3⁹.

On '*We know that*', see *Note 27*. p. 124.

On '*begotten of God*', see *Note 15*, p. 77.

On '*sinneth not*', see *Note 6*, p. 36.

'*he that was begotten*'. Some MSS read 'keepeth himself'
(as *AV*), in which case '*he*' means the Christian. The better
reading gives '*keepeth him*' (*RV*, *RSV*), '*he*' being Christ the
'only begotten' Son of God, and '*him*' being the Christian.
The believer cannot 'keep' (preserve) himself when evil assails;
his only confidence is that the indwelling Christ will purify
his motives and strengthen his will, and so in the hour of
testing will preserve him from the powers of evil (cf. Jn 10²⁸,
17¹², ¹⁵, 1 Pet 1⁵). His prayer is, 'Defend us thy humble
servants in all assaults of our enemies; that we, surely trusting
in thy defence, may not fear the power of any adversaries

through the might of Jesus Christ our Lord' (Collect for Peace, *Book of Offices*, p. 25).

'*toucheth him not*'; rather, 'does not lay hold of him'. The Devil cannot drag him back into slavery (see *Note 25*, p. 114).

5¹⁹. '*we are of God*'; born into His family, we belong to God (cf. **4⁴**, Jn 8⁴⁷).

'*the whole world*'; see *Note 7*, p. 38.

'*lieth*' = 'lies passive in the grip of'.

'*the evil one*', see *Note 12*, p. 56.

5²⁰ᵃ. '*is come*'. Once again, as his letter closes, John reminds his readers that the faith and life of the Christian are based on the historical fact of the incarnation and the abiding presence of Christ in his own experience.

'*understanding*', i.e. 'insight'. Through the Paraclete, His 'other self', Christ guides us into all the truth (Jn 16¹³) and gives us insight into the full meaning of that revelation of God which Jesus gave in His earthly life.

'*know*' = 'have personal experience of'; see *Note 8*, p. 43.

'*him that is true*'; i.e. God who is the ultimate Reality, the only real God, and who is known to the Christian as He really is (Jn 17³; see *Note 4*, p. 25).

'*in him that is true*'; i.e. intimate union with the only real God (see *Note 10*, p. 48).

'*even in his Son*'. Omit '*even*'; there is no corresponding word in the Greek. Translate '*through* union with His Son'.

5²⁰ᵇ⁻²¹ should, perhaps, be read as the last verse of the Epistle.

'*This is the true God*' has often been taken to refer to Christ; if so, it is a striking declaration of His divinity. But the sense of the whole paragraph suggests that we should paraphrase as follows: 'This—the God about whom I have written in this letter, the God who is Light and Love, the God who has been perfectly revealed to us by His Son and with whom we now live in personal and intimate union—is the real God; God as He really is.'

'*and eternal life*'. This refers back to '*we know him that is true*' in verse 20a, and means '*and* [to know the real God is to possess] *eternal life*' (see Jn 17³).

'*idols*'. John says, 'Have nothing to do with any sort of idol'; and to him an '*idol*' was any person or thing, any idea or ambition, which could draw men away from the worship of the one real God, who has been made known in Jesus Christ. It was unlikely that any of his readers would be tempted to worship the image of a pagan god or goddess, but there are more subtle forms of idolatry. John has already warned them against those pagan desires and ambitions which these deities symbolized (see comment on 2¹⁶). To compromise with pagan standards of behaviour is to erect idols in the place where only the real God should be worshipped. In this sense, the worship of the old pagan gods is still fashionable—the worship of Mammon the god of material success, of Minerva the goddess of science, of Fortuna the blind goddess of luck, to mention only a few of our modern idolatries—nor must we forget that, in the realm of thought, many modern '*ideologies*' are only new forms of old '*idolatries*'. The Christian must constantly be on guard against the unconscious worship of such substitutes for God.

John also has in mind the 'new theology' of the heretics who have rejected the basic doctrine of the incarnation. Compromising with pagan conceptions of God and Gnostic speculations about His nature, they are worshipping a God of human invention; a substitute for the one real God. This also is idolatry. If John were writing today, he would have strong words to say to many who, using the language of religion and propagating their beliefs with religious fervour, are in fact worshipping God-substitutes, and gaining converts from the rank and file of the Church. Nor must we ignore the fact that, even in orthodox circles, there is a danger that we may invent a God who is like what we *want* Him to be, and worship a deity of our own imagining (see J. B. Phillip's *Your God is too small*). Moreover, it is even possible for the means of grace to supplant the God of grace in our order of priorities; excessive reverence for the Bible, the Church, the Ministry, the Sacraments, the Saints is another form of idolatry. Only by constant reliance on Christ the Guardian of his soul (5¹⁸, 2 Tim 1¹²) can the Christian be preserved from any rival devotion which would draw him away from worship of the real God, the God and Father of our Lord Jesus Christ.

NOTE 27. CHRISTIAN CERTAINTY

We live in an age of bewildered uncertainty. Man, as a cartoonist has drawn him, is an insignificant little fellow, contemplating with an air of baffled perplexity a gigantic question mark. In the realm of ethics, for instance, many people no longer recognize any absolute standard of morality by which they can, with some certainty, distinguish between right and wrong. When asked his advice on a vital point of morality, one of our eminent thinkers replied, 'We are all groping. You must grope with the rest of us'. But the fundamental cause of this widespread uncertainty is that modern man, by and large, has lost his *religious* certainty. He is no longer sure of God and therefore he is no longer sure of anything. Are we proclaiming to this bewildered generation, with unshakable assurance, a divine Saviour who can change perplexity into certainty, spiritual frustration into victory, and the futility of living into the glory of eternal life? A faith which has not such a certainty at its heart cannot sustain those who hold it, convince enquirers who long for it, or pierce the scepticism of those who deny it. It was because John Wesley could say of his 'conversion' experience, 'An *assurance* was given to me that Christ had taken away my sins, even mine, and saved me from the law of sin and death', that he and those who shared that assurance became flaming evangelists, taking the world as their parish. But the first Methodists were only rediscovering the apostolic certainty of the early Church. How unshakable, for instance, were the convictions of Paul; see Rom $8^{16-17,\ 38-9}$, Phil 1^{19}, 2 Tim 1^{12}, etc. But nowhere in the New Testament is this note of certainty so dominant as in *1 John*.

Some of John's readers were losing the certainty of their faith. The dispute between their leaders about the basic truths of Christianity had unsettled their minds. They were no longer sure of their Saviour and their salvation. It was to restore this certainty—that they may '*know*' (5^{13})—that John wrote to them and to all who need such reassurance. His message centres in one tremendous, basic certainty: that '*we know that the Son of God is come*' (5^{20}), that He came '*in the flesh*' as the human Jesus (2^{22}, 4^2), that He lived and died as the incarnate Son ('*by water and blood*', 5^6), and that He came to be our Saviour by destroying '*the works of the devil*' (3^8). It is no wonder that, in every age, this faith has been met with incredulity and denial. Indeed the man who is not first staggered by it, who accepts the startling doctrine of the incarnation without any 'honest doubt' and searching questioning, must be lacking in imagination and blind to its far-reaching significance. His is an unthinking faith, easily held and just as easily lost. He does not know the difference between credulity and certainty. John challenges us to think through our doubts by studying the evidence that can re-establish our certainty. '*We know* this, and this, and this' he writes, and so, in verse after verse, he masses the evidence, piling certainty on certainty until his final conclusions are almost irresistible.

K

(*a*) *The evidence of reliable primary witnesses.* In his opening and closing paragraphs, John reminds us that Christianity is not a matter of speculation and guess-work about God and life's mysteries, but of divine self-revelation. It is based on the historical fact that God's Son has come to earth to be our Saviour (5^{20}); that He was heard and seen and handled by reliable eyewitnesses (1^{1-3}; see *Note 1*, p. 15). After His resurrection, and by the inspiration of His Spirit, they reached the unshakable conviction that He was none other than the very Son of God, the divine Saviour of men (4^{14}). This is the testimony of reliable witnesses and interpreters, and we accept it and put it to the test in our own experience.

(*b*) *This evidence verified in personal experience.* Accepting Christ's revelation of God and His loving purposes towards us, we commit ourselves to Him as our divine Saviour. God then gives us a share in His own Spirit (3^{24}, 4^{13}, 5^{7-10}) and we have an immediate assurance of His presence in our hearts. We *know* that we are now 'begotten of God' (2^{29}) and that we belong to His family (3^{19}, 5^{19a}). We *know* that we are living in intimate union with Him, He in us and we in Him (2^5, 3^{24}, 4^{13}, 5^{20}). We *know* that His Spirit gives us insight into His nature and will (2^{20}, 5^{20}) and that we know and experience God as He really is (2^3, 5^{20}). So we *know* that already we possess eternal life (3^{14}, 5^{13}) and that one day we shall be like Christ Himself (3^2).

(*c*) *This experience is tested and confirmed by our behaviour.* We *know* that we are living in God and sharing His eternal life by the supernatural quality of our own conduct; by the fact that, through His indwelling power, we are living far beyond our human resources. So our Christian certainty is finally established when we *know* that we are obeying God's commands ($2^{3-4, 29}$), loving Him more and more perfectly (2^5, 4^{16-17}, 5^2) and our human brethren too (3^{14}, 4^{20-1}, 5^2); when we *know* that we are winning our victory over inward sin (5^{18}) and coming to imitate Jesus in our daily behaviour (2^5).

Herein, therefore, is our certainty; that Jesus Christ, the divine Saviour who exercised His saving ministry in Galilee and Judea and has continued it through the centuries, is *my* Saviour; that even now He is at work in my heart, enabling me to live the eternal life of God —the life of 'perfect love' to God and man—and giving me mastery over inward sin and victory over external evil; and that He will continue His transforming work within me, until I fully share His nature and His life. This is the certainty which we offer to our bewildered contemporaries.

Second Epistle of John

Introduction

THIS Epistle is a pastoral letter, written by the Elder to a particular church in his 'diocese' (see comment on verse 1). His condensed references to *1 John* show that his readers are already familiar with that letter, in which he attacked the teaching of the heretics who have left the Church and are now engaging, with some success, in a rival missionary campaign. The heretics, however, have not yet reached the church to which John is writing. He sends this brief letter to urge its members to be loyal to the true faith and to boycott the false teachers when they put in an appearance. No more need be said in writing; he hopes to visit them soon and speak to them more fully.

Commentary

1. '*The elder*'; see Introduction to *1 John*, p. 2.

'*the elect lady*'. The Greek word for '*lady*' is '*kyria*' and it was sometimes used as a proper name. Some, therefore, think that *2 John* is a private letter to a devout lady whose name is Kyria. However, the fact that this '*lady*' is loved by *all* true Christians (verse 1), the references to her large and scattered family (verses 1, 4, 13), and the whole message of the letter, make this very unlikely. Most modern commentators agree that '*the elect lady*' is the personification of the local church to which John is writing, that '*her children*' are the members of that church, and that '*the elect sister*' of verse 13 is the sister church where John is now ministering.

'*in truth*' means more than that John loves them 'in reality' or 'most sincerely'. As we have seen in *Note 4*, p. 25, '*truth*' in John's writings means the ultimate Reality, God Himself as He has been revealed in Jesus Christ, who also is 'the Truth'. What John means is that he loves his readers with a more than natural affection; with a love which originates in God Himself, the ultimate Reality whose very nature is love. This is the love which all Christians must have for each other (see *Note 11*, p. 52).

'*that know the truth*'; i.e. 'who have saving knowledge of God as He really is, through their self-committal to Christ'— in a word, 'all genuine believers'.

On 'knowing God', see *Note 8*, p. 43.

2. '*For the truth's sake*'; better, 'because of the truth' (*RSV*), i.e. the Paraclete, the Spirit of Truth, who '*abideth in us*' (see comments in 1 Jn 2²⁷, 3⁹) and who '*shall be with us for ever*' (cf. Jn 14¹⁶), to inspire within us this genuine Christian love (Gal 5²²). Real Christian fellowship is only possible to those who share the life of Christ through their common possession of His Spirit. Any failure in Christian love reminds us of the lovelessness of the heretics, whose profession of Christianity was based on a lie (1 Jn 2²²⁻³) and who were inspired by Antichrist (1 Jn 4³).

3. '*Grace, mercy, peace*'. By coincidence, Paul uses the same words in his salutations in 1 Timothy 1² and 2 Timothy 1², but with a significant difference. Instead of expressing the *hope* that we shall receive these divine gifts, John *assures* us that these blessings '*shall be with us*'.

'*Grace*'. It was Paul who established this great word in the vocabulary of the Church, and gave it a distinctive meaning: 'the love of God, taking the initiative in redemptive action' (see *KG*, p. 14). John uses the word only here and in John 1¹⁴⁻¹⁷, but whenever he writes of the 'love' of God (Jn 3¹⁶, 1 Jn 3¹, 4¹⁰, ¹⁶, ¹⁹) he means what Paul means by the '*grace*' of God.

'*mercy*'. Only here in John's writings. For its meaning here, see 1 John 1⁹, Luke 18¹³, Ephesians 2⁴, Hebrews 8¹².

'*peace*'. Jesus said, 'My peace I give unto you' (Jn 14²⁷; cf. 16³³) and Paul wrote of the incomprehensible 'peace of God' as standing sentinel over our hearts and minds (Phil 4⁷). See *KG*, p. 15.

'*from God the Father*'. Here follows that full confession of faith in the incarnation which John has stressed in *1 John* (see *Note 14*, p. 68).

'*in truth and love*'; two words which sum up John's message

in this brief letter. The blessings of which he assures us come
through our union with and devotion to Him who is both
ultimate Reality and Love.

4. John begins his message, as Paul did in seven of his letters,
with a word of joyous congratulation.

'*I rejoice . . . found*'. It seems that some members of this
church have recently visited John and given him a report
about its spiritual life.

'*certain of thy children*'. The report was not altogether good;
only *some* of the members are loyal in faith and conduct (see
comments on verses 5-6). It is unrealistic to imagine that the
early Church, by comparison with the Church of today, consisted of none but saints. Even a cursory reading of the letters
of Paul and of John would correct such a judgement.

'*walking in truth*'; cf. 'walking in the light' (1 Jn 1[7]) and
'walking even as he walked' (1 Jn 2[6]); see comments and also
KG, p. 66.

'*received commandment*'; see comment on 1 John 2[3].

5. '*new commandment . . . beginning*'; see comment on
1 John 2[7].

'*love one another*'; see *Note 11*, p. 52.

6. '*this is love . . . commandments*'; see comments on 1 John
5[3], 3[23]. This insistence that Christians should '*walk in*' love,
as in truth (verse 4), follows the statement that *some* of the
members of the church to which John is writing—only some
of them—are living the life of obedience. Internal discord is
troubling this church, though the apostate missionaries cannot
be held responsible for it, since they have not yet arrived. John
urges his readers to grasp the fact that brotherly love is a basic
requirement of the gospel as it has been proclaimed from the
beginning, and that failure in love is culpable disobedience to
God. Let them settle their quarrels at once, so that with a
united front they can meet an even greater threat to their
fellowship in Christ (see next verse).

7. '*For many deceivers*', i.e. impostors who will try to 'lead
astray' the faithful; see 1 Jn 2[26], 3[7]. John explains why he
has stressed the importance of brotherly love. The propa-
gandists of the 'new theology' (see p. 3) have 'gone forth

into the world' (see comment on 1 Jn 4¹) and at any time may reach the church to which John is writing.

'*they that confess not*'. On their heretical opinions, see comments on 1 John 2²², 4², and *Note 14*, p. 68.

'*the antichrist*'; see comments on 1 John 2¹⁸, 4³ and *Note 13*, p. 67.

8. '*Look to yourselves*'; cf. Mark 13⁹. Paraphrase: 'Before the heretics arrive and propagate their specious arguments against the incarnation, examine yourselves as to whether you understand that doctrine and are absolutely convinced that Jesus Christ was both real man and divine Saviour.'

'*wrought*'; better 'worked for' (*RSV*). Some MSS. read 'ye' for '*we*', but the latter is probably the true reading, and refers to John and his fellow teachers in the 'diocese'.

'*full reward*'. Our critics often accuse us of being good in order that we may earn substantial rewards in heaven, and contrast this calculating goodness with the disinterestedness of the higher pagan, who is good because to be good is good in itself. It is true that Jesus often promised rewards to the faithful (Mt 5³⁻¹², 6¹⁻⁶, ¹⁶⁻²¹, ³³, Lk 14¹²⁻¹⁴), but this does *not* mean that He encourages us to calculate what courses of conduct will be the best paying propositions and what present sacrifices will result in the largest dividends in the hereafter. No, there is nothing of self-seeking in the motives of the real Christian. The reward of service here is opportunity for greater service hereafter (Mt 25²¹), the reward of present sacrifice is the capacity for fuller sacrifice, the reward of giving is to have more to give. In a word, the supreme reward which Christ offers is that 'eternal life' which consists in sharing the life of God Himself, becoming like Christ, and living the life of perfect self-giving love to both God and our fellow man. This is the '*reward*' John does not want his readers to lose— that 'eternal life' of which he has written so fully in *1 John*.

9. '*goeth onward*', 'goes ahead' (*RSV*); not 'transgresseth' (*AV*). We might almost translate, 'is progressive'. John is thinking of the proud claim of the heretics to be 'advanced thinkers'—'theological progressives' who have left behind their kindergarten faith in the incarnate Son (see p. 4).

'*and abideth not*'. John does not condemn *all* progressive theological thinking. In his Gospel, does he not record Jesus's promise that the Paraclete, His other self, will guide us to an increasing understanding of Himself and His gospel (Jn 14²⁶, 16¹³)? In *1 John*, has he not shown that he himself is a 'progressive', leading us on to new insights into the meaning and the implications of faith in Christ? What he condemns is any 'advanced thinking' that leaves the real Christ behind, which claims to supersede Christ's own teaching about Himself, the nature of God, and the conditions on which eternal life is given to men. A 'new theology' which abandons as out of date the basic truths of the primitive faith is plain heresy.

'*hath not God . . . Son*' seems to refer to 1 John 2²³⁻⁴ (see comments).

10. There was much travelling along the roads of the Middle East, and hospitality to visiting brethren was a recognized Christian duty (see 3 Jn 5-8, Rom 12¹³, 16¹⁻², 1 Pet 4⁹). 'But', writes John, 'when these pseudo-Christian theosophists reach you and claim hospitality on the grounds that they are "Christian" missionaries, you must shut the doors of your homes in their faces. You must even cut them dead in the streets of your town, and refuse to recognize them'. We are reminded of John's refusal to stay in the public baths when Cerinthus entered them (see p. 69). At first, this insistence on a complete boycott, this harsh intolerance of theological opponents, may well puzzle us. Does not John tell us, again and again, that the supreme duty of the Christian is perfectly to *love* both God and his brethren? But we must remember the critical situation with which John is dealing. We need not doubt that, when these one-time Church leaders began to voice their denial of the incarnation, the Elder reasoned with them in the spirit of earnest Christian love, pleading with them not to undermine the faith and endanger the unity of the Church, or to excommunicate themselves from its fellowship. Only when they proved adamant in their rejection of the basic truths of the Christian faith and ethic, and made plans to win both orthodox Christians and pagans to their pseudo-Christianity, was John driven to adopt an attitude of forthright intolerance. If, throughout Asia Minor, this caricature of Christianity triumphed over the apostolic faith and its standards of morality, the result would be disastrous. How grave John felt the danger to be we can judge from his policy of boycott, and from the fact that he called the heretics 'antichrists'(1 Jn 2¹⁸, 4³).

In John's day, Christianity was still in its formative period; its great Creeds were not written, and its faith as a world religion was not established, until the fourth and fifth centuries. Very rarely, since then, has the Church in any country been threatened by heresy so widespread and deadly that the survival of Christianity in that nation has become a critical issue. Very rarely, therefore, has the attitude of fierce intolerance towards heretics and the ruthless policy of excommunication been justified, though at times, alas, they have been practised. In our own time, however, the Confessional Church in Germany, under the leadership of Niemöller, must have felt the relevance of John's words to their own situation when they faced the threat of the 'German Christian' movement created by the Nazis. An even more critical situation might arise in Western Europe, if a powerful country whose avowed policy is one of militant atheism were to gain political control—a situation in which the Church might be forced to choose between a policy of collaboration and compromise, and the Johannine policy of complete boycott. Whether or not such a crisis ever occurs, John's words should remind us that, at all costs, the fundamental truths of Christianity must be defended and preserved against every form of apostasy.

11. To be even on speaking terms with them would suggest to the weaker brethren and to pagan onlookers that these travelling heretics were justified in using the word 'Christian'.

12. If anything John has written in his Gospel is still puzzling his readers, even after his simplified summary of that teaching in *1 John*, he will discuss these difficulties with them when he pays them a personal visit.

'*paper*'; probably made of papyrus, rather than the more expensive parchment.

'*your joy*'; see comment on 1 John 1⁴.

13. The members of the church from which John is writing send their Christian greetings (cf. Rom 16²¹⁻³, 1 Cor 16¹⁹⁻²¹, Phil 4²¹⁻², etc.).

Third Epistle of John

Introduction

The Letter

THIS Epistle differs greatly from *1* and *2 John* in subject matter. It is a private letter from Presbyter John to Gaius, a trusted friend who seems to be a well-to-do layman in a church somewhere between Ephesus and the outskirts of John's 'diocese'. There is serious trouble in a neighbouring church which is probably a little nearer to the border of the province. John writes to inform Gaius of the trouble, which is concerned with discipline rather than with doctrine. He accuses Diotrephes, not of any tendency to heresy but of insubordination and ecclesiastical ambition.

This was an age of transition in organization. Up to now, the supreme authorities in matters of leadership, doctrine and discipline had been the apostles, and the intimate disciples of the apostles—some of whom (like John) could also claim to have had personal contact with Christ. But John was now an old man. After his death, who would lead the Church in Asia Minor, and what would be the nature of his authority? A similar problem had to be faced throughout the whole Church, and a solution must be found for two reasons: to maintain doctrinal orthodoxy in the face of aggressive heresy (*1* and *2 John*), and to maintain discipline when the central authority of the Church was repudiated by such ambitious demagogues as Diotrephes (*3 John*). It was to safeguard the faith and enforce discipline that, in the next decade or two, the system of rule by bishops was established. The letters which Ignatius, bishop of Antioch, wrote to certain churches in Asia Minor during his last journey to Rome (*c.* A.D. 107) show that by this time the larger churches in the province were governed by local bishops, assisted by presbyters and deacons. It may well be that John was already preparing for this transition to the new system; indeed Demetrius may have been his nominee for a future bishopric. Meanwhile, he must deal with Diotrephes.

Why was it written?

Our interpretation of *3 John* suggests the following tentative reconstruction of the events which caused it to be written:

John had sent a group of missionaries to the outskirts of his 'diocese' to evangelize the pagans, and to visit and encourage the local churches—and *perhaps* to deliver a copy of *2 John* to each Christian community. Reaching the church to which Gaius belonged, they had been cordially welcomed and generously entertained by him. Continuing their tour, they had come to the church of which Diotrephes was the presbyter or 'minister in charge', and had asked for hospitality. The truculent presbyter had called a Church Meeting at which he had repudiated the right of Presbyter John to exercise ecclesiastical authority over a church so distant from Ephesus, and had proposed that no hospitality should be given to his travelling agents—and *perhaps* that his letter (*2 John*) should be returned, unopened. The proposal was carried by a majority vote. Some members, however, remained loyal to John, voted against the resolution and offered the missionaries the hospitality of their own homes. Diotrephes so far exceeded his authority as to excommunicate the loyalists from the Church. Upon this, the missionaries returned post haste to Ephesus to present their report to John. Before the whole church, they told of the fidelity and generosity of Gaius, and of their very different treatment at the hands of Diotrephes and his party. This brings us to the point where John wrote *3 John*.

John must enforce discipline. He decides to send his missionaries back to the offending church, this time under the leadership of Demetrius, a man who is respected throughout Asia Minor. Demetrius is entrusted with a letter which he is to hand to Diotrephes with the request that it be read at the Church Meeting; a brief letter whose contents we can guess (see verses 9-10). This time the missionaries are to be welcomed and given all necessary hospitality. Diotrephes is rebuked for repudiating John's authority, and ordered to restore to the fellowship of the Church those whom he has excommunicated. If John's instructions are not obeyed, he will pay them a personal visit and deal with the offenders, lovingly but firmly.

On their way to their destination, Demetrius and his companions are to call at the home of Gaius and hand him a letter (*3 John*) in which John informs him of what happened to the missionaries after they left his hospitable home on their previous visit. In case Diotrephes proves adamant in his rejection of John's authority, he asks Gaius to be so good as to provide the missionaries with enough funds for their return journey to Ephesus.

Commentary

1. *'The elder'*; see Introduction to *1 John*, p. 2.

'Gaius'. John has a deep affection for this devout and wealthy layman; three times he calls him *'Beloved'*. It was a common name, and there is no reason to identify him with the Gaius of 1 Corinthians 1^{14}, of Acts 19^{29}, or of Acts 20^4. According to the not very reliable *Apostolic Constitutions* (4th century), Gaius became the first bishop of Pergamum, the church which is mentioned in Revelation 2^{12-17}.

'love in truth'; see comment on 2 John 1.

2. *'prosper'* (cf. Rom 1^{10}, 1 Cor 16^2). John has no doubt about Gaius' spiritual prosperity; therefore he can pray that his business will also prosper, for he knows how to use his money as a Christian. John also prays that his physical health will continue—or does he mean 'improve'? Has Gaius been over-taxing his strength in the Master's service?

3. *'brethren'*; the missionaries who have recently returned to Ephesus (see p. 134) and given a glowing report of Gaius' faith and conduct which has given John cause for great joy.

'thy truth', i.e. the truth of thy life, which means the same as *'thou walkest in truth'* (see comment on 2 Jn 4).

4. *'my children'*. All the faithful Christians of his 'diocese' are John's *'children'* (see *1 John*) and many of them have been converted under his ministry. Perhaps Gaius also is one of his converts. No wonder his heart is full of joyous thanksgiving to God, as he thinks of this magnificent Christian layman. After all, the real strength of the Church lies in a consecrated laity who witness to the pagan world by the vigour and intelligence of their faith and by the splendour of their Christian behaviour.

5. When John sent out missionaries from Ephesus, he seems to have urged them to observe certain rules which were based on those given by Jesus when He sent His disciples on tour (Mk 6[8-11], Lk 10[4-12]). They were to travel light, carrying only food and money to enable them to reach their next stopping-place on the great Roman roads of Asia Minor. The travelling public, however, was badly catered for in the matter of inns, so that private hospitality was most desirable. The itinerary of missionaries, therefore, was so planned that they travelled from church to church, using each church as a centre for evangelistic activity in its neighbourhood, and being entertained by the members of that church during their stay. When they moved to the next church, they were sent forward by their hosts with enough food and money for the journey. It is in this matter of hospitality that Gaius has rendered signal service to John's missionaries, most of whom were '*strangers*' to him. This is a '*faithful work*', says John; 'this conduct is the living out of your faith in and devotion to Christ'. Perhaps Gaius had remembered the words of Jesus: 'I was a stranger, and ye took me in' (Mt 25[35]). Certainly he is living up to the highest tradition of Christian hospitality to travelling '*brethren*' whether or not they are '*strangers*' (cf. Heb 13[2]).

6. '*bare witness*'. In glowing terms the missionaries had told the Ephesus Church Meeting ('*before the church*') of the gracious service of '*love*' which Gaius had rendered to them (see p. 134).

'*thou wilt do well*'. John begs his friend to treat Demetrius and his companions even more generously, and for a special reason (see later).

'*set forward*'. This practice of sending forward missionaries on their journey was an established custom in the early Church. The verb is translated 'set forward on a journey' in 1 Corinthians 16[6], [11], 2 Corinthians 1[16], and Titus 3[13], and 'bring on the way' in Acts 15[3], 20[38], 21[5], and Romans 15[24]. C. H. Dodd points out that though the actual meaning of the verb is 'to give a person a send off', a study of the above passages suggests that it had come to include the idea of defraying the expenses of the travellers (*CHD*, p. 160). Verses 6-8 will provide the preacher with a fitting text for a sermon on Overseas Missions Sunday. John reminds us that, when we have accepted and trained workers for the mission field, we must not only hold Valedictory Services for them; we must regard ourselves as financially responsible for the maintenance of their work.

'*worthily of God*'; i.e. in a manner befitting the fact that these men are God's messengers, about God's business (cf. Mt 10⁴⁰).

7. '*for the sake of the Name*'; cf. the joy of the apostles that they were 'counted worthy to suffer dishonour for the Name' (Acts 5⁴¹). The '*Name*', of course is 'Jesus Christ', whose name is 'above every name' (Phil 2⁹).

'*went forth*'. What a contrast to the 'gone forth' of 2 John 7. We should translate 'have gone forth'. John refers to the missionaries who have just arrived at the house of Gaius and handed *3 John* to him.

'*nothing of the Gentiles*'. The word translated '*Gentiles*' means 'pagans by religion', not 'Gentiles by race'. We now see why John urges Gaius, on this occasion, to exceed his past liberality. In contrast to the 'begging friars' of the pagan cults (*CHD*, p. 160), John has instructed his missionaries not to ask pagans for money, either on their journeys or at their evangelistic meetings. Nor must they accept free lodging in any but Christian homes. They come freely to *offer* a Saviour; not to collect subscriptions for the missionary work of the Church. All that they would beg the pagans to *give* is the response of faith to Jesus Christ. If therefore, for the second time, they are refused hospitality by Diotrephes and his party, they will have little food and money for their direct journey back to Ephesus. John asks Gaius to be so generous as to provide them with extra funds for such a contingency.

The pioneer work of the great Missionary Societies has always been financed by the sacrificial giving of the home Church. Only when converts from paganism have been gathered into the Church have they been invited to make their own contribution to the maintenance and extension of the work. Today, in many countries overseas, the native Church has become quite or almost self-supporting, and is now organizing and financing its own missionary work in the 'hinterland'.

8. '*fellow-workers*'. John reminds Gaius (and our own hearers) that, though he may not be called to be a preacher of the gospel and a missionary, by his generous support of those who are so called, he has joined the honoured ranks of those who are '*fellow-workers with the truth*'; i.e. with Christ who is the Truth, the revelation to men of God as He really is, and so fellow-workers with those who proclaim His gospel to the world. It is on this high level of appeal that we must call our people to sacrificial giving to the missionary work of the Church.

9. '*I wrote somewhat*'; better, 'I have written a brief letter' (see p. 134).

'*Diotrephes*' was probably the presbyter in pastoral charge of this unnamed church (see p. 133).

'*loveth to have the pre-eminence*'. The Greek verb so translated is a compound of two verbs, and is found only here in the New Testament. The second verb is used in Colossians 1^{18}, where Paul says that Christ is the Head of the Church and that only He has the right '*to have the pre-eminence*' Such great leaders of the Church as Paul and John never forgot this; they acted as Christ's representatives in a spirit of devotion and humility. But Diotrephes was a small-scale and ambitious ecclesiastic, who was determined not only to lead the church, but to dominate it. He was a 'little Pope', who wanted to run the affairs of the church as if it belonged to him. Again and again Jesus warned His disciples against the sin of wanting 'to have the first place', to claim the highest honours, to sit in the best seats, and to 'lord it' over their fellows (Mk 10^{37}, $^{42-5}$, Lk 14^{7-11}, 22^{24-7}, Jn 13^{3-15})—but it is doubtful if Diotrephes ever preached from these passages. Egoism *is* sin (see *Note 5*, p. 35), and ruthless ambition can work terrible evil in the life of the Church. An arrogant ambitious churchman, whether he is a minister or a layman, can lower the spiritual vitality of a church, drive immature converts out of it, and ruin its witness to the outside world. The man who has an outstanding gift for leadership must ever guard against this lust for power and position. He is only fit to be the leader of a church if he is the humblest man in it, 'the servant of all'.

'*receiveth us not*'; 'does not acknowledge my authority' (*RSV*). In refusing to receive the missionaries from 'headquarters'—and, perhaps, the letter from John which they carried (p. 134)—Diotrephes was repudiating the right of John to exercise pastoral responsibility over a church so distant from Ephesus. Ambitious demagogue that he was, he insisted that *he* was in charge of the church, rather than Presbyter John—a man who was not even an apostle, who was almost senile, and who knew next to nothing of the local situation. Under *his* leadership, he claimed, the Church Meeting was capable of managing its own affairs, maintaining the doctrinal orthodoxy of its members, and organizing its own evangelistic campaign among the pagans of the neighbourhood. As we have seen (p. 133), this was the sort of situation which, in the near future, made necessary the establishment of the system of rule by bishops, presbyters and deacons.

10. '*if I come*'. If Diotrephes and his party ignore John's instructions and again refuse to entertain his missionaries, he will pay a personal visit to the church. He will remind the offending presbyter and his party of all that was said and done at the previous Church Meeting. He takes it for granted that his presence, and this exposure of the delinquent presbyter, will restore discipline, and that those recently excommunicated (see below) will be reinstated in membership.

'*prating*'; better 'babbling'. The word stresses the fact that the wild charges brought against John are empty and baseless.

'*them that would*'. The loyal minority (see p. 134) had insisted on opening their homes to the missionaries, despite the warning of Diotrephes; whereupon the presbyter arrogated to himself the right to act on behalf of the whole Church, and excommunicated them. The missionaries would immediately return to Ephesus.

11. This verse, surely, does not mean that John is afraid that Gaius may imitate Diotrephes and those who have followed his lead. Perhaps, as in verse 10, John is giving Gaius the gist of what he has written to the offending church in his brief letter (verse 9). They must recognize that the real issue between John and Diotrephes is not one of personal prestige, but of the difference between '*good*' and '*evil*' behaviour. If they '*imitate*' (follow the lead of) their ambitious presbyter, they will show that they do not really belong to God (see comments on 1 Jn 3[9–10]) and have not really '*seen God*'; i.e. had intimate experience of Him (see comments on 1 Jn 3[2] and 3[6]); in a word, they are not genuine Christians.

12. '*Demetrius*' is not to be identified with the silversmith of

Ephesus (Acts 19²⁴). He was possibly one of John's assistant presbyters in that church. John seems to have placed him in charge of the missionaries on this difficult assignment, and has done so because he is a Christian whose worth is recognized throughout the 'diocese'; he *'hath the witness of all'*. Surely even Diotrephes and his fellow-malcontents will be predisposed to listen to him. But more; *'the truth itself'* testifies to his character. He 'walks in the truth' (see comments on verses 3-4) and so his whole manner of life declares that he is a devout Christian. And to provide a threefold witness, John adds his own word of commendation; *'we'*, i.e. John and his colleagues at Ephesus, can unreservedly vouch for his character. We are reminded of the 'epistles of commendation' (2 Cor 3¹) which Paul provided for such people as Sister Phoebe (Rom 16¹⁻²) and Tychicus (Col 4⁷⁻⁸).

'thou knowest'. Gaius knows that John would not give such a testimonial to Demetrius, if he were unworthy of it (cf. Jn 21²⁴ᵇ). We are sometimes embarrassed when an applicant for employment or a position of trust—someone who is almost unknown to us—asks us as responsible Church officials to write a 'testimonial' for him. John would faithfully deal with such a request.

13. Cf. 2 John 12a.

14. *'I hope'*. John is looking forward to visiting the church to which he has sent *2 John* (2 Jn 12b), and also the home of Gaius.

'Peace unto you' was the usual Jewish greeting, which could become a mere formality. In the same way, how many English people remember that 'Good-bye' really means 'God be with you', and what significance has 'Yours truly' at the end of a business letter? But since the Risen Jesus had said *'Peace unto you'* in the Upper Room (Jn 20¹⁹), these words must have had a deeper significance when used by Christians (see comment on 2 Jn 3, and cf. Jn 14²⁷).

'The friends' means more than 'the brethren'. Gaius has personal friends in Ephesus and they send greetings to him. John has personal friends in the church to which Gaius belongs, and he asks Gaius to give his personal greetings to them *'by name'*, individually (cf. Jn 10³).